# GET OVER

# DIVORCE

# LIKE A

# MAN

ALEXANDER PIERCE

ALEXANDER PIERCE

# Contents



ALEXANDER PIERCE

# I. MISTAKES

## 1. If you look in the mirror and don't see value, women won't see it either!

That's how we all suffer—a beautiful and quiet day, which in a few seconds turns into a nightmare. From where you didn't even see the clouds a few minutes before, you wake up in the middle of a storm.

Actual separations occur on clear days, not when we argue and shout at each other. But, like any man in a divorce situation, he made all possible and impossible mistakes. Why? Because in himself, the man thinks he's worthless.

But let's take them one at a time. If a woman tells you that she is leaving you and you tell her, "okay, do what you want," you send the wrong message. It's not exactly what you want to convey. What should you do? Ask her if she's sure she wants to, and if she says yes, tell her it's not what you want, but if she changes her mind, she should look for you. Do you see any difference? There is.

 If you pass in front of her house on your daily journey, you go around elsewhere. I don't care how, but you find a solution, at least until the madness ends.

It happens that after a few days, she comes home, you talked, you discussed. Sounds decent. It's just that I know what that talked and discussed means. It means you tried to negotiate reconciliation. Specifically, tell me what you want me to do to love me, and I will do it. Women are crazy about this attitude, and they get wet instantly.

I'm sure she didn't come back after she left because you behaved like a personal servant. Does Miss needs heat? I'm going to turn on the boiler. Does she want chocolate? I'm going to bring chocolate. Does the lady want declarations of love? I don't know, but I do them anyway.

What can I say? I'm sure women are dying for attitudes like this. Remember that women don't fall in love with waiters at the restaurant, they just tip them. Behave a lot like a personal servant, and you will see why the attitude of a slave does not attract women. Speaking of Richard Cooper, treat her like a star, and she will treat you like a fan. And you don't want to be left with just one autograph while she leaves with another man.

Then you find out that your wife cheated on you. And you have little self-esteem to put an end to everything and say that you deserve more. To look in the mirror and say to yourself, " I'm a man of value, and I deserve a woman who doesn't cheat her husband." Please look in that mirror and slap yourself.

You say you don't have the strength to stop. What to stop? She stopped for you too. You just have to accept that and go on with your life. And do you know what to do? Determine your worth as a man. Make a realistic assessment and see if you deserve something in this world, or all you can do is hope that a woman who has made an irreparable and unforgivable mistake will take pity on you and get you back.

Do you think I'm harsh with you when I tell you you're begging for her mercy? Because that's what you think you deserve. And it may be true, I have no idea, that I don't know you, I'm just saying that it's unfortunate to think that you deserve so much from life.

How to get over it? How to forget it? Well, you have to become a man of value. To get to look in that mirror and see a man who deserves more than a woman like her. Do you think you are asking too much?


**2. What do you do when she gets cold with you?**

But like any relationship, it went through a period of cooling. It's normal, it happens to anyone, and not just once. And it's not even a bad thing. If you know how to manage these periods, they can be a good thing.

It's just that what do we do when we feel she's not so affectionate anymore? We try to show her affection. And this is a terrible strategy because we want to do it. We do it in the hope that she will return the gesture and show us the same affection. And when you do that, you smell desperate, and women can feel desperate men.

Do you know what we don't want to understand? That this distancing of her that we feel is not because we did not show her affection. On the contrary, for one reason or another, she simply needs a little space. She needs her life to exist beyond you. No matter how much you like a person, if you stay with him/her 24 hours a day for several months, at some point, you get tired of him/her.

Ahhh, and not to forget. Some women do this on purpose to test you. It's a good way for them to figure out what kind of man you are, and I don't judge them at all for that.

But what did ”Tom” do when he felt he was losing her? He puts his feelings on a silver tray. Why does a man do that? As I said above, he does it in the hope that she will do the same. And what does she do? She sends him emoticons.

Well, what did you think, "Tom"? That she'll fall in love with you just because you told her you loved her? A woman's attraction to you doesn't take into account how much you love her.

Do you want me to translate what you did? The subliminal message sent by you is this: "look, I love you, love me back!". What woman doesn't instantly fall at your feet when you pray for her to love you? The answer, none.

And yet, what do you do when you feel like she's not so in love with you anymore? You let her miss you. You give her space to breathe. You let her see that life away from you is not so pleasant, and if your relationship was a good one, she would return.

Just like cats. The more you try to keep a cat, the more it will run away. When you leave her alone to do what she wants, and you don't force her to come to you, you will see that she comes alone and puts herself in your lap.

The opposite of love is not hate, it is indifference. And indifference hurts much more than hatred.

## 3. The biggest mistake you can make with a woman.

I have no words to describe how important what I am going to say now is. If I ask you now the biggest mistake you can make with a woman, you will answer something completely different. But if you don't take it seriously what I'm going to tell you now, then there's no point in reading on. All you do is waste your time. And anyway, you don't understand that women are different from us men.

Because you can make many mistakes with a woman, but you often expect what you do to have a result. But there is a mistake with serious effects, yet its consequences take you entirely by surprise. And if you've ever been abandoned, and at the moment, you didn't understand why then read carefully.

The biggest mistake you can make with a woman is to bore her, never feed her need for emotions, never go through all the states. Never allow her to be nervous about you, to wonder what you are doing right now, what you will do next. Never give her a chance to be jealous.

You mean, like, sometimes she's upset? Yes, to upset her sometimes. You forget that seduction is a game that never ends. It is possible that you did this thing initially, after which, when you saw yourself in a relationship with her, you thought that from now on, you have to give her security.

And you turned into that predictable man next to whom women get bored. You attracted her with an exciting story, with emotions, with enthusiasm to meet someone new in her life, and now what are you doing? You show her a house taken with a 30 years loan, a car that you will end up paying over five years, children, a secure job, a sofa that you will be lazy as introverts every night, and a vacation, all-inclusive, once a year. And, let's not forget, Saturday is a day to clean the house, and Sunday is a day to lick the wounds after a tough week, that sounds very exciting.

You attracted her with an exciting story, and now you expect her to behave as if you are retired. And so, one day, you wake up with the famous phrase "you know, I met someone at work," and you don't understand how she could kick everything you built together for someone who doesn't give her anything.

Don't you think that person is giving her something you haven't given in a long time, something like emotions? That the person is making her always think of him? That the person isn't boring, like you? Do you have any idea how important it is for a person driven by emotions to give her the chance to go through several states? No, you have no idea.


## 4. Is it normal to cry as a man?

In short, yes, it's normal, but never do it in front of a woman or your children.

And this is where the controversy begins. Because the modern man is not afraid to express his emotions in front of a woman, but when it comes to the attraction between a man and a woman, no one cares if you are a modern man or not.

I'll start with the most straightforward part. It is normal to have emotions, feelings, or sometimes feel overwhelmed by the things around you. It is good to realize what your feelings are, be aware of them, and analyze them. But it's not okay to let yourself be overwhelmed by emotions.

It's good to eliminate emotions in some way. It's up to you how you do it, a punching bag, a sheet of paper, or even crying.

Why? Because no matter how hard feminism tries to convince us that a man should cry, it does not change the fact that for hundreds of thousands of years of evolution, there was a period when crying was a sign of weakness.

And if you are lucky, you will find women who will tell you this straightforward. They will tell you that they are not attracted to men who cry and do not want to see their man overwhelmed with emotions.

Let's say you have an excuse when someone close to you dies. But otherwise, it's not okay to see you crying.

I suffered it myself, many years ago, when I allowed myself to let a few tears run down my cheeks because I had the impression that no one was seeing me at that moment. I remember the reason very well, it was not insignificant, but it is irrelevant.

And, as I let my feelings overwhelm me, my wife came and surprised me in my moment of weakness. She listened to my problem and even told me it was the first time she'd seen me cry. She even asked me not to cry in front of her anymore.

If you think about it, her behavior sucks. The man who will become your husband is crying, and your only problem is not to cry in front of you. And I would be very upset about this if I didn't understand it perfectly today. Why?

Because women hate weak men, women are made to reject weak men. And that's why I think some women make fun of weak men, to show others that such behavior is not okay.

My wife didn't tell me why not to cry in front of her. She just told me not to. And you will find many women who will tell you that too. But, at the same time, you will find everywhere in today's press and in the movies that you see that it is okay to cry, express your feelings, and behave exactly like a woman.

Some women will say that they like to see a man who knows how to express their emotions. And I'm convinced I'm not lying. But there is a big difference between what a woman likes and what sexually attracts her. And you have to be the one with the sexual attraction. Otherwise, you're just friends.

In recent years, there has been a fierce struggle to redefine the idea of masculinity. Please pay attention to one thing: those who try to change the notion of masculinity are those who do not have it. You will find women talking about redefining masculinity, and you will find those men who can be characterized in many ways, but not real men.

You will never find truly masculine men to complain that masculinity needs to be redefined.

The past few days have marked more than 75 years since the Normandy landing. Do you think those men weren't scared? Do you think they didn't want to cry all the time? Do you think they didn't want to tell their wives or friends how they felt? But they did their duty and were not influenced by feelings. Today you are put on the wall if you tell a man not to cry in front of a woman.

And yes, today's men wear jeans with their ankles exposed, including in winter. And yes, they behave like women, but you know what? I see more and more women taking action and saying bluntly that this is not the kind of man they are attracted to.

Because yes, socially speaking, such a thing has become acceptable. And yes, today, it is socially acceptable to cry in front of a woman. But that woman will never get wet when she sees you crying.

Recently have appeared men's club where they hug. Heterosexual men sit for 2-3 hours, hugging as many as possible in huge beds. Do you think their wives are still attracted to them? Do you think that a woman will feel safe to be led by such a man?

Because no matter what nonsense the Media teaches you, your role in a family is still the same. You need to be a pillar that does not bend under pressure, and makes the family feel protected.

And how do you want to be an attraction between you and your wife as long as you behave like a woman? That's why you end up in sexless relationships, that's why you end up being cheated on, and that's why women are the ones who initiate divorce in 70% of cases.

Yes, this campaign that teaches us to show our emotions will continue. And it shall come to pass, that a man shall weep in front of a woman, and shall not be judged. It may no longer be considered a sign of weakness.

But no media campaign will change the fact that women are not attracted to crying men. No media campaign will make your wife's DNA blind to the fact that you behave like a woman.

And I repeat it for the thousandth time, for those who still don't know what women want. Women want men! They want your courage, they want your self-control, they want your calm, they want your strength. They want to know that you will not be overwhelmed by emotions if things get complicated and solve the situation. They want to know that you can protect them and your future children.

You can try to play the role of the modern man and see what happens. Then, if you get burned playing with fire, I'm waiting for you to explain why it's not good to overlook over 200,000 years of evolution. It only costs you a divorce to learn that you are not brighter than all those who were men before you.

## 5. Is it normal to have a sexless marriage?

It's normal because it happens very often. It is suspected that 20% of couples are in such marriages. The even better question will be if a sexless marriage is healthy? No, no and no. Lack of sex is the best way to destroy a marriage.

Officially, a sexless marriage means that the two spouses have sex no more than ten times a year, which is awful.

And what's even sadder? Besides being rare, it's also bad. It's hard for me to believe that if you have sex every two months, you have quality sex. Usually, there are erection problems in men, it is possible that she is not highly aroused. She will not be delighted with your mega 4-minute performance.

If at the beginning of the relationship you received oral sex almost daily, now you need a letter of intent, an appointment, and a feasibility study. Quite different from what you see in porn movies on the internet. Because yes, you watch porn movies.

A poll conducted by the Huffington Post says that 75% of men are bothered by being in a sexless marriage. 50% of them say that they would not have married if they had known that they would end up in such a marriage. And I understand them. After all, you are a man, and you have physiological needs.

And when your needs are not met in marriage, you solve them elsewhere, for example, on the internet. Only some men end up cheating because of these needs. They stay in that marriage because they love their wives, but they have needs. And that's not the kind of marriage you'd like to be in.

Others become frustrated by the lack of intimacy. No relationship is healthy when one of the two is frustrated with the other. This is how disputes come out of nowhere, passive-aggressive behavior, and, in general, this is how happiness dies in a relationship.

But there are couples where neither he nor she has a very high libido. And they are not interested in sex. Is such a relationship healthy? Again, the answer is no. And that's because many women don't have libido problems in general, they have libido problems when it comes to their husbands.

Do you know what "Fifty Shades of Gray" is about? Many of us call it deviant behavior or something that only low-income women would find attractive. It's hard to believe that your wife would be interested in such things. And yet, those movie theatres weren't full of lowly women. They were full of all kinds of women.

I assure you that many women in sexless marriages have seen "Fifty Shades of Gray." I assure you they read the book too. Why? Because they are sexual beings, just like you, and this is the female version of porn movies, as if women don't watch porn movies.

And if she has low libido for you, it does not mean that it will be the same when someone else appears in her life. It does not mean that a new co-worker, a new neighbor, a new man in your circle of friends will not increase her libido. And, further, you realize for yourself how a healthy marriage without sex is.

Because sex is what binds a relationship, whether we like it or not, that physical act binds us more than we think. I remember an expression I heard often. "Over time, sex turns into respect." The expression always comes from those who live in such relationships.

Well, I think if sex turns into respect, then you've just become best friends in the world. That doesn't change the fact that we also need intimacy in our lives. And with your wife, you want to play the role of intimate partner, not just a respected friend.

What to do? Become the man to increase her libido. To realize that the woman does not want to have sex just because you proposed to her but needs foreplay. She needs you to get her in a particular state of arousal. And that's your job.

What is very important to remember? When you say that your wife does not want to have sex, please add the expression "with you." Because your wife has nothing against sex, it's just that she's no longer attracted to the prospect of having sex with you. And, many times, it's your fault.


## 6. Did you steal someone else's wife, and you expected to trust her?

I don't like to tell you negative things. But the truth is, you lied to yourself and closed your eyes too many times. And today, you pay for those lies.

I don't want you to see everything in black, just as I don't want you to see everything in white. I want you to know the reality, and the fact is that if your wife cheated on her ex-boyfriend to be with you, she would cheat on you to be with someone else.

Why? Because she considers infidelity to be acceptable. Why wouldn't she do it again? After all, you know what kind of woman she is. Why wouldn't she do the same to you? Are you so special that she has no eyes for anyone else in her life? Let's be serious!

But you have to realize one thing. These are the consequences of lying to yourself. And it was an important lie.

And I don't think you've ever thought about that. I don't think you had a problem trusting her. I don't think you've ever wondered if she won't cheat on you as she cheated on her ex.

Because you believed her words, you listened to her as her ex was a bastard and had many flaws. And you thought you weren't like him so that situation couldn't happen to you. You're special. You're one in a million. You are precisely the kind of man she is looking for, so you will never be in the situation of her ex-boyfriend or husband. Sounds nice, but you're lying to yourself.

All that matters is that when she was not satisfied with her boyfriend, she decided to cheat on him. She could very well break up with him, then look for someone else. But no, she chose to be unfaithful. His flaws don't matter much. The fact that the ex was unfit for her was a good excuse for her to leave him. There is no good excuse for cheating.

And maybe you're the ideal man for her. And perhaps she found her happiness with you. But do you know something? Life is long. Statistically speaking, if you are 30 years old, you still have at least 50 years to live. Much can happen in 50 years. Very much. Are you sure you can keep her happy for 50 years?

And you know something else? One of the reasons a woman cheats is boredom. Did you think you wouldn't get bored at all in the next 50 years? Did you think you would be a perfect husband for all those years? Let's be serious, no one is perfect.

And if you had the pleasure of watching her call her boyfriend or husband and lie to him that she does something else, but sex with you, then it is called that you are foolish. If you saw her lie to him and never put yourself in his place, you played yourself.

You can say that you were blinded by beauty or by sex. You can say you were immature, young, or ignorant. You can tell it any way you want. I would call it stupidity. And the situation could be even more comical if you didn't pay for your mistakes now. So I'll call it a lesson.

So I'll end with some advice. Stop stealing someone else's wife or girlfriend! If she sees that she is interested in you, don't make long-term plans. You can sleep with her, or you can ignore her, your decision. But that woman is not what you want for a relationship. It's a simple rule that keeps you from being deceived. And there is no excuse for this rule.

## 7. Did you give your wife a chance to be a sexual being?

We men make a big mistake. We label women in two categories: good women and less good women. And I think it's a mistake because I'm firmly convinced that the two women are, in fact, the same person. If you have already reached divorce, at least you know where you went wrong, if you have another chance to escape, then pay attention to what I will tell you next.

I do not know how it is that a man's wife is a good girl in the vast majority of cases. Almost every time. How can your wife have sex just for pleasure? What does it mean to have erotic fantasies as you have? Sex for her is more like a reward for you, for being a good boy and taking the garbage often, and for the rest, just for breeding. Otherwise no. Otherwise, women are asexual beings who "are not interested in sex."

Those women you see on the net are something different, people have gone crazy, and people don't go to church anymore, that's why they do what they do. Your wife is not that kind of woman. God forbid! What does it mean to slap her on the ass, what does it mean to dominate, to overwhelm her with your masculine energy, to tie her to the bed, to subdue her? Your wife only wants the missionary position once every two weeks, and if you insist and deserve it, the oral sex you want. And only if she feels like it.

Your wife has an organ explicitly designed for sexual pleasure. Precisely, the clitoris does not play a vital role in reproduction. Its role as an organ is to detect the stimulation of the area and to create pleasure. And your wife's clitoris doesn't know if you took out the trash, if you were a good boy, or if you deserve that thing because you like it. He will produce pleasure if it is stimulated.

And at least once a month, during ovulation, women are overwhelmed by hormones. Their body tells them that they are fertile, and it is the ideal time for reproduction, so it will secrete hormones that will make the woman more easily aroused and eager for sexual contact. Also, her hormones don't know if you took out the trash.

Many women have read the books and seen the movies in the "Fifty Shades of Gray" series. The books were sold like hot pancakes, the movie theatres were packed. Is it possible that women also have erotic fantasies and want to be dominated? Is it possible that your wife is attracted to this kind of interaction? Wanting to be dominated by a real man so that she can become highly feminine? Possible.

But if she knows you will judge her for having sexual desires, then she will never open up to you. She will never have the courage to tell you exactly what her fantasies are. And I assure you that you also like her fantasies. If you've ever had sex with her under the influence of alcohol, you've noticed that she was much more open to new things, including that thing you like. Why? Because alcohol kills inhibitions, without thinking about the fact that you're going to judge her for it.

You could have that fantastic sex every time, but you only hindered yourself when you didn't treat your wife like a sexual being. Did you have the impression that she would come to you to ask you to pull her hair, to dominate her?

What to remember? That you have to give her a chance to say no. Tie her up and let her refuse you if she doesn't like it. Dominate het, and if she doesn't feel comfortable, she will tell you. Pull her hair, slap her on the ass, and don't stop until she asks for it. Subdue her and overwhelm her with your masculinity, and most importantly, don't judge her when you see pleasure on her face. Because you will see pleasure, take it as a sign that you've finally found out what kind of world you live in. Yes, women love sex as much as you do.

## 8. Not sure she still loves you? Don't ask her that!

If you have to ask her, then the answer is no. You feel that something is wrong. Otherwise, you would not ask yourself this question. But the question is awful, and it shows so much insecurity on your part that I'm almost sure I know why she doesn't love you anymore.

Why do you want to ask her that? You're aware that a negative response from her would upset you, right? The insecurity in you pushes you to ask a question meant to calm you down. You want to hear her that she still loves you, that everything is fine, that you can rest easy, the relationship will go on.

Don't ask the question because you are curious if there is still love between you two. Ask the question because you need to calm down that strange feeling you have had for a while, which does not give you peace and that you fear might be true.

Have you ever seen in James Bond movies the main character ask this question? No.

Bond has two strengths that you must learn.

First, Bond does not need the validation of the woman next to him. That is, he will be the same man, whether she still loves him or not.

Second, he doesn't need to ask her if she still loves him. He realizes himself. Because he's much more attentive to what the woman is doing than to what that woman is saying. So, if the woman tells him she loves him but treats him with disrespect on the same day, do you think that's love?

And yet, what do you do? Look at her behavior and answer your question. Has her behavior changed?

When you come home from work, is she still excited to jump into your arms, like she used to? If you don't kiss her anymore, does she try to kiss you on her initiative? If you don't contact her anymore when you're not together, does she write to you first? If so, does she write to you because she misses you and wants to see how you are doing or just to remind you to buy bread when you come home?

When was the last time she came to you just because she felt the need to hug you?

If we started with questions like this, ask yourself the most crucial question: are you happy? Is that what you want? Would you be happy to know that this will be your relationship for the next 30 years?

And if you conclude that she no longer loves you, don't panic! Having in our blood the attitude of men who solve problems, we tend to fix things, to do something. It's great that you want to fix things and make her love you again, but make sure you know what needs to be done.

If you have the impression that you have to overwhelm her with your attention, you are on the wrong path if the first instinct is to buy her flowers or gifts.

Calm down, don't try to compensate for her more withdrawn behavior towards you. Keep reading this book and see where you went wrong in the relationship. And only when you are sure that you know what you are doing wrong is it time to act. But you have to do it with your head.

## 9. Did you fulfill all her wishes, and she's still not happy?

Frustration. Lots of frustration. You did everything you knew you had to do, and it's still not good. No matter how much you struggle to make her dreams real, she's still not happy. You feel like you speak different languages , and there is no translator. You feel your wife distant, and you are afraid of what is worse for your relationship, so you try to show her what a wonderful husband you are, and yet her only reaction is frustration.

Frustration is the only thing you have in common now.

More frustrating is that, although it is in your nature to solve problems, you cannot find a solution to this problem. And you feel that the deadline is coming over you, because yes, there is a deadline, the day she will leave you. The idea of losing her scares you, so you try even more challenging to make her happy, and the only reaction you arouse in her is even more frustration.

At one point, you give in and show your helplessness, saying something that should never come out of a man's mouth: " Tell me what I need to do in order to make you happy, and I will do it! ".

The expression could be reformulated very well in the following way " I don't know how to be a man in a relationship, please show me how to behave. "

You can ask any woman, but I don't think you'll find one to tell her she wants to hear this from the man she's in a relationship with because women don't want to teach you to be a man. They might teach you, but they won't! Because if they have to teach you to be a man, then you've lost their respect. And what's the point?

Let's say you get a new boss at work. That person comes from another department and has no idea what you are doing, so he has to start over and ask you to help him learn everything you already know. You help him learn, you treat him well, I'm sure you respect his position, and you may even become friends, but I don't think you respect him as a professional.

The first time you encounter an obstacle, and as your superior, he will try to impose himself in front of you, I am sure that you will look at him with contempt. You will think that you have taught him everything, and professionally speaking, you are far above him. And that's not respect.

Think, instead, that the new boss comes from the competition and knows everything you know, but because he was successful at his former company, he was brought here to implement new ideas, already tested and which have given excellent results. The numbers don't lie, and his numbers look much better than your numbers.

He knows precisely what strategy he has to implement, and he can implement it himself, but if the people in your department would help him, the results will be seen much faster. If you have not already realized, you will respect this type of superior as a professional, not only for the position.

And if you don't understand why I wasted so much time with my example, then I tell you this: the woman next to you must respect you. She wants to see that you know what you have to do. She doesn't want to teach you. She wants to follow someone she respects because he knows exactly what he has to do. If the situation becomes complicated, she wants to be the person who has to learn from that situation, not the one who has to teach others.

What do you have to do in this situation? I don't know. You have to learn to decipher what she wants from you because it's clear that what you've done so far hasn't worked. Many reasons can lead you to this situation, and you need to see precisely who is to blame in your relationship. All I'm saying is, today, don't use that expression.

And for everyone to hate me, I hope that this passage is also read by those who say that communication is essential in a relationship. Yes, at the beginning of the relationship, communication helps a lot, but in the end, you may find that you speak different languages because women and men communicate differently.

The mistake is that you come to believe that your relationship is based on communication, you expect her to tell you every time you do something wrong.

Why is it a mistake? Because feelings are not logical. You are waiting for a rational response to her emotions. You will not receive it. Sometimes you don't receive it because she doesn't know why your actions frustrate her either. She also understands why she feels this way but does not want to offend you by telling you that you didn't behave like a man.

And once in a while, she knows why you're frustrating her, she doesn't mind telling you directly that you're misbehaving, but she just doesn't want to play your mother. She doesn't want to be the one to educate you, to raise you, to help you become a man. Maybe she already has a baby and doesn't want you to be the second. Perhaps she needs a father for her child, not another child to wipe her nose.

And sometimes, you will not get the correct answer because she may not care about the relationship anymore. Maybe she's already given up.

And to hate me to the end, I say this: communication is essential as long as both people involved in a relationship want the relationship to work. Unfortunately, sometimes it happens that one wants that relationship more than the other. That's why it's not good to insist on going to couple therapy at the end of the relationship because only one of the two wants that relationship to work.

Often, the second person is there just because they don't want to be seen as guilty of divorce just because they haven't tried couple therapy. It is much easier to say after two or three sessions that the therapy does not work. After all, it's not the person's fault anymore, she/he tried.

## 10. Do you want to know what kind of relationship you will have with her? Look at her parents!

Jumping over thousands of jokes about mothers-in-law, your ex-wife's mother should have been an essential source of information when you decided to turn your girlfriend into a wife.

Why? Because no matter how much we try to minimize this aspect, your wife will behave very similarly to her mother. Your wife will imitate what she saw at home, just like you replicate what you saw at home.

You must understand that people who complain about what I write here argue that not all people are the same. In reality, they are called generalizations because they are generally valid. But you are my guest to believe what you want and prove me wrong. After all, you only put your future at stake, nothing important.

And yes, I think your wife doesn't look like her mother. Maybe she looks like her father, perhaps she has different behavior. And what about education?

If the father's role was played by a weak man who does not know the definition of self-respect, do you think it will be easy for your wife to respect you? If she saw in her mother that the husband must be harassed with all kinds of nonsense, how do you think she will behave with you?

Suppose her father has repeatedly cheated, and her mother has become a monument of jealousy. Do you think you will escape without knowing what it means to have a jealous wife? On the other hand, if her mother cheated countless times, do you think she taught her daughter to be loyal?

If she grew up in a family where "my mother was the rooster in the house," it would be a torment for you to play the role of the man in the relationship, and she will constantly try to undermine your authority. As a real man you are trying to become, you are lucky because there is an excellent chance that she will have a relationship with a weak man. After all, that is the pattern of the man she knows.

It is possible that she will not be attracted to strong men, just as you, as a strong man, will not be attracted to a very masculine woman. But you still have to be careful.

How does your mother-in-law spend? Doesn't it seem strange to you that your wife spends almost like her mother? If, on the other hand, your mother-in-law always manages to put money aside, you're in luck.

What I want to tell you is that whether you are divorcing and realizing that there are things you did not consider before marriage, you are simply preparing for a new relationship, or you are at the stage where you are thinking of you ask your girlfriend to become your wife, her parents must be analyzed and the results assumed.

The idea is that your wife lived in that family for many years and learned how to be. That can be a good thing, or it can be a bad thing. Maybe your in-laws are lovely and have passed on to your wife only solid values and a chosen education. In that case, you can call yourself lucky.

However, there is a chance that she did not learn everything she saw wrong from her parents. There are situations when her mother has made wrong decisions in life, and she condemns those decisions. Maybe she grew up with her grandparents, maybe she was educated by another person, perhaps she simply had to live with the consequences of her mother's mistakes, and she understood that this is not the best way to lead your life. There are women like that.

What you need to understand is that if she was very close to her grandmother, or maybe she spent her first seven years with her grandparents, away from her mother's infidelities, for example, you can't breathe a sigh of relief by betting that she received her education from her grandparents. It's a straightforward way to make sure that person shares your values, and it's essential to consider.

If the woman you want to have a relationship with condemns her mother's mistakes, then you're in luck. If she doesn't condemn them, I wish you success in proving that not all people are the same.

And to expand on the subject, if you find out that her best friend is cheating on her husband, but she doesn't condemn her, where do you think she puts fidelity and monogamy on her priority list?

Or do you think it doesn't bother her to see infidelity at her close friends, but it's different with you? She would never deceive you because….. (insert stupid reason here)…. It amazes me how special you are and how this can never happen to you.


**11. Do you still know how to be a man, or are you afraid of confrontation?**

I think our parents poorly educated us. I believe we have been sedated by society to become non-conflicting. We are sold the idea that giving up is a virtue, that settling a conflict by simply giving in is a desirable deed and denotes social intelligence.

We, as men, have become more and more castrated by society, and the results are starting to show.

First of all, I find it hard to believe that this expression, "the smartest gives up", has been around for a long time. I think a few hundred years ago, if you were arguing with someone, you weren't doing a virtue of giving in to him, and I'm sure that if that person offended you, you were defending your honor.

I know that it has not been widely practiced in our places, but if someone insulted you, you would challenge him to a duel in the past. I think we used the fist, the scythe, the ax, or any other tool to show the one who offends you that he didn't choose the right person to offend.

You had to be willing to risk your life for your name, your status. If you wanted the world to respect you, then you had to be willing to take action. I have never heard anyone in history brag that he was offended, but he left him to be because that is the Christian thing to do, and there is no point in letting the situation escalate.

And I don't think this was due to a lack of intelligence. Even though schools did not exist, culture and education were lacking, not intelligence. I think, however, that much more emphasis was placed on the respect received from others. And I think men were men, and they were educated from father to son that they should not be trampled on.

There are two possibilities. I often hear "the smartest gives in" when the one who says it no longer has arguments to continue the dispute, in which case, not the smartest has given up, on the contrary, some of those who use the expression have an IQ below average.

When I argue with someone, if the person I'm arguing with is defeated and I hear the expression "the smartest gives up" or "there's no point in arguing with you because you won't understand", then I instantly become happy. I know I won. I imposed myself in front of him, and he gave up. That makes me feel strong, and I like the feeling.

It's just that, more recently, since I started reading people and the interactions between them, a situation like the one above makes me sad. And that's because I look at the one who gives in to how he uses this new virtue acquired to rationalize his capitulation.

His brain couldn't accept the idea that he gave in to me, that he didn't dare to defend his point of view, so he had to put his head on the ground and tacitly accept my idea. He can't accept that he was trampled on. His brain conceals his cowardice, dressing her in a virtue that will help him accept himself as a man, which will allow him to sleep peacefully at night in the fantasy he has created.

Why am I saying this here? Because the one who gives in is not the smartest, he is only the weakest man. And women know that. This expression is most often heard in women. Yes, I know it's stupid to argue with women, but what to do? I'm conflicted, I like to argue. I also have a favorite expression: "if I know I'm right, I'll die to prove I'm right!".

That doesn't mean I'm automatically correct. I was often shown that I was wrong, in which case I admitted defeat. At the same time, I can't help but think about how many times I wasn't right, and yet I won because the person I was arguing with gave up for fear of conflict. And here I don't care who's right, I care who dominates who.

Why did I bring up women? Because women don't argue logically, they argue emotionally. When they can't find arguments to counter you, they know they gave in to you because you dominated them. They will use the expression, but in themselves, although they will never admit it, they will know that they have just let you dominate them.

I want to say very clearly that I do not advise you to carry an ax after you on the street for situations when someone looks at you badly.

I am trying to warn you that when you argue with a neighbor from a parking lot, for example, although you will feel very modern and proud of the way you settled the conflict if you give in to the neighbor and use " the smartest gives in", know that your wife will consider you a weak man.

Your wife knows you weren't brave enough to face your neighbor, or the one in front of you at the store queue, or the one who challenges you in traffic. Your wife can't respect you if you don't respect yourself enough not to be trampled on by anyone.

And don't forget that women always wonder if you can protect them. If you can't stand the neighbor of the block for a parking space, will you be able to protect her when, late in the evening, some strangers get their hands on her ass? Do I need to tell you that your wife's attraction for you just went down the drain?

And if you are one of those sad people who complain that women do not want a quiet and loving man and prefer only the so-called "bad guys", know that from those bad guys, you will never hear the expression "the smartest gives up". And this is a good reason why women prefer them.


## 12. Financial stability is a man's duty!

Has anyone told you are the new finance minister? No? Then you're unlucky because, for your family, you're that finance minister, whether you want to or not. And unfortunately for you, it is a function with many sacrifices, a lot of responsibility, and a single reward, that of having a happy family.

At the same time, many families have divorced because men have not emphasized their role as the family's financial pillar.

Now I will turn into your father, because he is the one who should have told you, with subject and predicate, the fact that you, and only you, are responsible for the financial stability of the family. Even if some of you do it late in life, it is still good to learn your responsibilities as a man.

And although the family consists of both husband and wife, the truth is that both bear the laurels of possible economic success, but you are responsible for avoiding failure. And maybe you tend to consider yourself unjust. Still, I don't agree with you, because that has always been the man's role, no matter that today, women are presented to us as independent, and you breathe a sigh of relief that you have escaped responsibilities.

Maybe if I talk to you about homo sapiens, it will seem very impersonal to you, so I'm talking about your grandparents. Because until recently, the roles of a man and a woman in marriage were still well defined. Your grandmother gave birth and cared for the children, maintained the household, and your grandfather procured resources. It was the man's duty for the family to have something to put on the table.

And this was not something established only in their family, but it has been happening for hundreds of thousands of years. It is in our DNA to provide resources to women, resources that women will use to raise children.

And yet, look at us today as we feel that if our wife has a job and is an essential provider of family resources, we are no longer the only ones responsible, and the burden is not just on our shoulders. We believe that hundreds of thousands of years of evolution no longer matter, just because women have their salaries.

It is essential for a woman to feel safe next to you, and this security includes several factors, including financial security. A woman needs to know that she has something to put on the table tomorrow. A woman needs to feel that if she obeys you and lets you be the pillar of the family, you are capable of being a leader.

If she constantly lives in uncertainty, the bills come monthly, and she doesn't know if she has anything to pay them with, do you think she will feel safe next to you? If you cannot ensure the family's financial peace, do you think she will consider you a suitable man for her and her children?

A few hundred years ago, if you couldn't raise resources, you couldn't find a wife, and your genes wouldn't reach the next generation.

I'm not talking about women here who only look at your money when they look at you. There are such women, and you have to learn to stay away from them. But, a quality woman will understand you when you have hard times. Maybe you lose your job, maybe you lose your business, maybe you have a period in which you can't bring home the money you used to bring. And that quality woman will be by your side and support you.

But do you know anything? That woman wants to see you do your best to rectify the situation. She wants to see you use all the time to find a new job, start another business, and overcome the difficult time you are going through. You need to feel that the most challenging time you are going through is just temporary. She needs to feel in control of the situation, ambitious, and determined to solve the problem.

Because if you are not in control of the situation, you are not the man she wants. If you have lost your business and all you do is complain of pity, then it is clear that its future is bleak with you. And why would she stand by you when all that is announced in the future are shortages and debts?

Suppose you work on a miserable salary and do nothing to improve your situation. How do you want a woman to remain attracted to you? Yes, they can stay with you, but it cannot be an attraction as long as all you show them is that you indulge in mediocrity. Women do not want mediocre men.

If she spends too much, it's your job to stop. We all want our wife not to miss anything, and most of the time, it's hard to turn her down when she wants something, but if you conclude that you make less money than you spend, then it's time to be very careful with your expenses. No matter what expenses you give up, you must impose yourself and ensure that you do not spend more money than you have.

And loans, shopping cards, or money borrowed from different people will not make her feel safe with you. It may not be instant, but her attraction to you will be affected by eternal debt in time. So whether you like it or not, you have an extra burden on your shoulders, whether you reconcile with your ex-wife or marry someone else.

And I want to clarify one thing, I'm not telling you here to fill it with gifts or that you have to produce vast amounts of money to satisfy all her cravings. No matter how much money comes into the house, you have to be careful to spend less or at most equal to that amount and always do your best to increase your income. I'm just saying to ensure the family's financial stability and always be concerned with creating prosperity.

And if you want, I'll be right, you're not the only one to blame for the financial situation. But do you enjoy the fact that she is also to blame as long as you wait in line at the notary to sign the divorce? Isn't it sad to know that no matter how reckless she is with money, it was in your power to avoid separation?

## 13. Learn to make decisions. Your wife doesn't want to be your mother!

"I don't know baby, what do you want us to do tonight?" Surely you know the expression, I'm sure you've used it many times. What you don't know is that this expression led you to divorce. Without realizing it, every time you used it, you packed a T-shirt in the luggage she left you with.

If it doesn't sound familiar to you, I remind you of the derivatives: "I don't know which restaurant to go to, where would you like it?", "I don't know what to order at the restaurant, order something for me too", "I don't care which t-shirt you choose, choose one, and it's okay for me too ". "Should I buy bread with or without seeds, what do you say?" and, in general, any situation in which she became your mother and had to decide for you.

I know it doesn't seem like an important thing, but guess what? If you knew what mistakes to avoid, you wouldn't end up in this situation, so admit that you have a lot to learn.

Have you ever wondered why a woman would want to be in a relationship with you? What does she have to gain? Suppose your answers are about your physical appearance. In that case, we are talking about sexual attraction, and you do not need a relationship for that. If your answer depends on how well you can satisfy her in bed, likewise, you don't need a relationship for that. And yet, why would she want a relationship with you?

There are many answers, but the one we are interested in today sounds like this: women want to be led, they want to know that you are the leader of the interaction, they want to see you able to make decisions, they want to see you able to do without them because they don't want to be your mother.

If they have a child, they want to know that you can be head of the family. They want to see that you are helping them.

And yet what does it matter if you don't know which restaurant to go to? It's just a restaurant! Yes, it's just a restaurant, but you missed a perfect chance to show her that you are a leader, you missed a perfect chance to make her feel safe. You missed an excellent chance to show her that you are a man she can count on, who can run a relationship.

And you feel good when the leader of the group you belong to is very good at what he does. Maybe you are a sales agent, and the marketing director is a born leader with impressive sales figures. This will give you confidence, and you will produce better results.

Maybe the new manager of the company is known in the market as being very good in management. This will give you all confidence in the company, and you will feel that the job is safe.

Maybe you have been moved to another department, but you know that your new direct superior is very good at what he does, so you set off confident that you will quickly learn the new job requirements. I don't think I have to give you a hundred examples to understand that a good leader boosts high morale to everyone around him.

This is precisely what a woman is looking for when thinking of a relationship, a good leader. And yes, not all women are the same, but most are looking for that. A man to lead the interaction. Why? Because if he doesn't lead the relationship, then she will have to lead him. And she can't respect a man who is waiting to be led in a relationship because he is no longer seven years old, he needs a nanny to raise him.

Respect is essential in a relationship. It is the only necessary ingredient. His disappearance usually foretells the end.

How could she respect a man who is not able to make a simple decision? Why would she want to babysit you? Why would she want to play your mother? Why should a man who voluntarily relinquishes his place in a relationship be respected?

Every indecision, every hesitation, every task transferred to her strikes deeply into her attraction for you and decreases the respect she has for you.

I offer you a little game, and here the women surely will hate me. Next time you are in this situation, you may choose A and B, but you know that the best decision is A. You are sure that she also knows that the best decision is A, but she made you choose. In that second, be a man and choose B, short and to the point, without trying to explain yourself.

You will notice that although she knows that the best decision is A, in most cases, she is okay with your decision because you made it quickly, without hesitation, and you showed confidence in yourself and your decision.

You can learn from this that it is not very important in a relationship if you choose Chinese or Arabic food, bread with or without seeds, a restaurant, or a terrace on the student campus. It is essential to lead, it is essential to give them the feeling that you are in control of the situation.

I hope I don't have to explain to you that if she doesn't agree with your decision, you don't have to be stubborn and go all the way.

Also, I hope I don't need to explain to you that if the decision is an important one, then you have to take your duty as a man seriously and take the best possible decision because you will have to assume the consequences.

If you were like me, you probably did all this because you didn't care. You didn't care where you went out on Saturday night, what restaurant you went to, what to order, or all sorts of such decisions that you saw as unimportant.

And I know you still see them as unimportant, but guess what? Conclusion: there are decisions, and your role as a leader is to make complex and trivial decisions. I assure you that they are just as trivial for her, but they are not her decisions to make.

So the next time she asks you, choose the bread with seeds, no matter how boring the subject seems to you, and stop giving her reasons to leave you.


## 14. What do women want?

Feminism has brought many benefits to women. Unfortunately, it has also brought many problems. These are becoming more and more obvious nowadays when you can no longer distinguish between the sexes when women are more and more masculine. Men are more and more increasingly feminized.

We are told everywhere that men and women are equal. No, we are not equal, for the simple fact that we are different and cannot be compared. It would be the eternal comparison between apples and pears.

What has been beautiful in the last 200,000 years since the appearance of homo sapiens has been that this difference between the sexes has created sexual attraction, which has led to the perpetuation of the species.

Our DNA today is victorious. He is the one who has survived for the last 200,000 years. Why do we try to deny it when it would be best to understand it? Let's see what the differences are!

Two hundred thousand years ago, homo sapiens appeared in East Africa. The man was visibly more prominent and strong than the woman, but that wasn't the only difference. The woman's body was adapted to create new human beings, while the man's body was adapted to survival. He was capable of both hunting and protecting women and children from the dangers of the African savannah.

If predators decided you were a good source of protein as a pregnant woman, you couldn't do much. If a foreign man decided that you were the ideal victim for his most recent rape, you didn't have much to say about it. Thus, women needed to be protected by men.

As a man, instinct told you to reproduce. That meant you had to find a healthy woman who could give birth to a baby and raise it.

Hence our part of DNA that makes a woman's physical appearance matter the most in sexual attraction. The brain tells us that that beautiful girl with big breasts is ideal for giving birth and raising a baby. Our DNA still doesn't know about makeup and silicone implants.

As a woman, it was easy to reproduce. Anyone could get you pregnant, but not everyone could protect you during pregnancy or raising your baby. And yet, during pregnancy, you needed the protection of a man.

If you didn't want to starve, it was a problem. You could not get food while you were pregnant or as long as you had a baby. It's hard to throw a spear at animals when you have a small child after you. So this role was taken by men.

And here came the first problem. Not all men were physically able to protect you in the event of an attack by predators or another tribe. Not all men were able to build a shelter to protect you as a woman during pregnancy. Not all men were able to hunt so that neither you nor your child would starve.

Thus, the survival instinct said that the woman must choose a strong and capable man, that "Alpha". Hence the DNA part of women makes them feel more attracted to dominant character traits than to physical appearance.

By the time she could reproduce, the woman not only needed protection and resources, but she also needed good genes for her future child. If she did not get the best possible genes, the future child would have been a Beta male, unable to hunt, reproduce and thus perpetuate the genes.

Women have been programmed for hundreds of thousands of years to look for the DNA of a winner, and today you are upset that she did not choose you, an obscure male who cannot take care of himself. No matter how much things have changed in the last 100 years, we cannot ignore 200,000 years of evolution.

The need to perpetuate the best genes made her attracted to an Alpha male. He attracted her with his courage, his ability to hunt and protect his family. Being the leader of the group, he was the first to go to war, the one who fought the most heroically, the one who killed the most enemies, and entered among the predators to get the most significant piece of meat.

Unfortunately, the alpha male also had a minor defect. Although he was the first to go to war, he did not always return home alive. If he returned alive, he would have to procure food for so many women with children that sometimes it was even difficult for him to cope with the situation. Thus, the woman woke up with a small child and no one to protect her, no one to find her food.

By the way, monogamy is a very recent concept, appeared in humans a few thousand years ago, in some cultures, it did not appear even today, so it is not written anywhere in your DNA that you will live with one partner all your life.

A male with Alpha genes, Alpha behavior, but stable in the long run and who always returns home to the family does not exist. So the woman was always in a dilemma because instinct told her to breed with an Alpha. Still, reason told her to choose a Beta male, who, although he didn't have a winning DNA, was quite capable of procuring resources stably and predictably for family survival.

Unfortunately for us men, this is why we do not understand what women want.

Women want something that doesn't exist. They want Alpha genes, courage, strength of character, they want a leader and a pioneer. But at the same time, they want a man they can count on, who is at home every night at a fixed time and who does not take unnecessary risks, always putting the good of the family first.

Do you see how all these traits clash? Since you have a regular job, do not take risks, and are predictable, you cannot call yourself an Alpha male.

This is why a woman marries that guy with a motorcycle and braids, then puts him to sell the motorcycle because it is dangerous. She tells him to cut his hair, to find a better job, after which she divorces him because she no longer feels attracted to him and leaves with a biker with hair.

In a woman's subconscious, there will always be a struggle between the emotional and rational sides. The emotional part is the one that reacts to the Alpha male behavior of the man, to the leadership traits, to the man's power. It manifests itself through physical, sexual attraction and appears instantly.

Like any man, a woman has a rational side, which tells her that she needs a man who owns or can procure resources to raise a child. The rational part, like the emotional part, leads to attraction, but it develops a little more complicated and is a rational attraction, not a physical one.

Let's not forget one thing, women are emotional beings. And no matter how rational they are, the emotional part will have a hard word to say. This means that no matter how much she loves you as a Beta male capable of maintaining her and ensuring a flawless life, she will always be sexually attracted to Alpha males, strong leaders, men in the true sense of the word.

So if you're a Beta and she left you for an Alpha, or you're an Alpha, and she left you for the financial security of a Beta, it's not necessarily her fault. It's your fault because you don't understand the attraction and didn't know how to get a little of each type of man.

You didn't know how to be the strong, brave, leader, strong in character, but at the same time financially stable, able to gather resources and support a family. And it's much easier today when we don't need to hunt.

## 15. Do you want a woman in your life, but do you need her?

No, you don't need her. Nothing kills a woman's attraction to you more quickly than the feeling that you need her, that you are afraid of losing her. So you will have to become independent from all points of view.

And this is not a two-dollar strategy, meant to influence women subliminally so that they give in 37.8% faster to your advances. No, it's a basic rule of masculinity, and it's damn important, especially nowadays when weak men surround us.

Okay, now let me explain why you don't need women. You, as a man, want something from a woman, sex, a relationship, a mother for your future child, a warm person next to you when you lie in bed in the evening, a conversation partner, or anything else. It's perfectly normal, and it's perfect that you want this. Humankind would go to hell if we men didn't want anything from women.

And women are pleased that we want something from them because they, in turn, want something from us. We want different things from each other, and this is where we start negotiating. Yes, in straightforward terms, this is how humanity developed from the beginning: the man asked for a womb to give birth to his descendants, and the woman asked for protection and resources for herself and the children.

But as I said, women have always looked for and will always look for the best genes to procreate. I guess you already understand that men with good genes don't have a problem attracting a woman.

As a woman, 100,000 years ago, it was easy to see who had good genes. You looked at who came back victorious from the hunt, who came back victorious from the war, or more simply, who was the leader of the tribe.

Today it is no longer fashionable to duel with members of a group to gain the right to reproduce with all the women in that group, and this is frustrating for them and us because women have to find another way to test who has good genes.

And the best solution they found to see what kind of man you were, was to watch how you behave. Because the man who has no problem conquering a woman behaves entirely differently from the one who is desperate not to lose a woman because he does not think he can conquer another. He behaves much more masculinely than the man who needs a woman's validation.

Believe it or not, women want physically and emotionally strong men. A real man must be strong when he has a woman in his arms and when he is alone. I understand I'm not working miracles here, and you won't start behaving like a real man tomorrow.

What I want from you, though, is to start analyzing the interaction between men and women, or even between teenagers in the park (the behavior is much more visible). When you see a man and a woman or a boy and a girl interacting, analyze his behavior and see if he can be categorized as "a man desperate to lose her."

Why do this? To understand where you went wrong with your ex-wife and to know how not to become that kind of man with another woman.

It's easy to recognize him. He is the man who makes all her wishes, who always likes her, who always agrees with her even if she says idiocy. He's the man who sends her a bouquet of 12 roses when they're arguing. And a gold chain, I had forgotten about jewelry.

He is the one who constantly assaults her with compliments, who constantly wants to hold her hand, who constantly asks her for affection. He is the person who always sends her messages, then holds her accountable for not answering. Or he points out that she never initiates contact and must always be the first to send a message.

He is the man who hurries to put the label of "relationship" to the interaction between the two, even if the two met only a week ago. To generalize, it is that man who puts self-esteem in second place in the interaction with a woman.

Why is it important to analyze all these things? Now analyze the response of women to the poor behavior of men. To see with your own eyes how little respect these men receive, how they let themselves be trampled on, to observe how angry women are with the behavior of these men. See with your own eyes how simple it is to kill a woman's attraction to yourself when you live in fear of losing her.

And in the end, once you understand how bad an attitude like this can hurt a relationship, you will have to understand that I am not asking you to be indifferent. I ask you to put your priorities in order and to put yourself first.

It's great that you want a woman, but you don't have to be willing to compromise too much to be with her. You can exist without its validation, and its mere presence on your arm means nothing if the relationship is not functional.

Nowadays, men no longer know how to put their foot in the door. They are afraid to say exactly what they want and what they think for fear of upsetting the women next to them. They are constantly told that a relationship means compromises, and they do not understand that there are certain things in life that they should not accept.

So, the next time when the interaction with a woman is not to your advantage, take a long look at her and admit that you want her. And you want it a lot because there is nothing more beautiful in this world than the female body. But realize that even though you want it, you don't need it, because you are number one on the list of your priorities.

# II. INFIDELITY

## 1. You know your wife's lover very well.

You will hear her talking about him. You will know what he does, what jokes he says, what nonsense he does at work, because statistically speaking, they met at work. You will know everything about him, the only thing you don't know is that he has a relationship with your wife.

Why? It's simple because she can't stop thinking about him, just as she couldn't stop thinking about you when you first met.

You will sit at the table in the evening, boring her with all the irrelevant details of the day that has just passed, and she will bring him into a discussion. What a joke he made, with who he argued at work, unnecessary details about how he does his job, sometimes details of his personal life. And you hear all this because, even though he's physically next to you, your wife is thinking about him.

And here I'm not talking about the talk of an evening or two. If it happens so often that you get to know many details about that man, then it's time to ask some questions.

How long will this last? Until your first gesture of jealousy. Will your jealousy stop her from being completely obsessed with the new man in her life? No, but it will make her realize that it's better to keep quiet around you.

So the worst idea now is to start showing her that you suspect her of infidelity. No, you have to shut up and listen. Listen and watch her smile when she talks about him. And, why not start looking for other signs of infidelity but without telling her anything.

Ahh, and let's not forget. That guy isn't her type. I'm not saying that. She says it herself when you start showing her jealousy. Because you're stupid, and you show that your wife's interest in that man bothers you, and she doesn't want to cause a scandal. And you believe it because, let me repeat, you're stupid.

What do you want her to tell you? That she would jump into his arms 5 seconds after you walk out the door? Of course not. She tells you that they're just co-workers, that she doesn't look at him that way, that the guy is married, as if that matters a lot or any other lie that will make you calm down and stop suspecting her.

If, for example, she met him in an unconventional place, she would not talk about him. But if they meet at work, she'll tell you absolutely anything about him because it's normal to know so many details about him, they're co-workers, right?

And in the end, an essential thing. All that I said above does not mean that your wife cheated on you. It just means she can't stop thinking about that man even when she quietly eats her soup at home. Maybe she's already cheated on you, maybe she's is going to cheat on you, maybe her attraction isn't shared by him, maybe who knows. All I'm saying is she's attracted to another man, not you.

## 2. Why do you think she deleted her messages from the phone?

Today's article is about accepting reality. You know the answer to that question, but it's hard to believe that it applies to your relationship. It wouldn't be the first time in your life that you tell yourself it won't happen to you.

And you know something? It's a pretty good strategy. Don't bother with all the nonsense in the world, and don't always live with worries. That is until it happens to you. Only then do you realize that some things should not be overlooked.

Today I will be short because I do not need to explain much, and you can not contradict me. Did you have the courage to decide what was going on? Did you pick up her phone and see that some conversations are missing? Do you know for sure that she is talking on WhatsApp or Facebook messenger with a co-worker and still you see that her phone is missing any trace of conversation?

The only reason a woman (or a man) deletes her messages is that she has something to hide. What do you think she has to hide?

What topics did your wife have with that person, and after she thought the best decision was to delete the conversation? Do you think they changed cake recipes? Do you think they talked about the weather? Do you think they talked about work? Let's be serious, you know what they talked about.

Put yourself in her place. If you were loyal to your wife and didn't flirt with other women, would you have a reason to delete phone conversations? No! Then stop apologizing and accept reality. If she deleted her phone call, then she's cheating.

It doesn't matter if she's just cheated emotionally or if it happened physically. It's the same. Even if it's a flirtation that led nowhere, it's still not ok. If she respects you, then don't flirt with others. And if you respect yourself, you don't accept her flirting with others. It's time to say goodbye.

### 3. Do you feel the need to check her phone? You are not in the right relationship.

Jealousy comes from a lack of self-confidence. It is not a disease, it is not a character trait, we are not born with it. Suppose a jealous man wins the grand prize in the lottery tomorrow, and the women start assaulting him. In that case, he miraculously gets rid of the disease of jealousy. But today, I don't want to talk about that kind of man.

Today I want to talk about men who are not jealous by nature but still feel wrong. Men are beginning to have doubts about their partner's loyalty.

And I want to be very clear. If you ever doubt that your wife is loyal to you, you should take that phone and check it. I'm just saying you're not in an ideal relationship.

The relationship is probably not what you wanted it to be for a long time. Most likely, she is no longer present in the relationship. I say you don't feel like she loves you anymore. I'm saying you probably don't get what you expect from a relationship.

If you find out she cheated on you, you can respectfully show her the door to get out of your life. You may not find anything on the phone and realize that it was all just in your head.

The question is: where did the question mark come from? Where did your doubt come from? Why did you end up losing confidence in her? If the culprit is your lack of self-confidence, then you have to work on it immediately. If the question marks come from her behaviour, then you have a problem.

This is a time when you have to analyze what happened and decide if you can fix something or if you have to break up.

Because unless you're jealous by nature, you had a good reason to lose faith in her. And you don't want a relationship with a woman you can't trust.

It's not good to give anyone total trust, but it's good to have a pretty big trust in the person you're in a relationship with. You don't want to live in fear of being deceived.

And if the relationship works, and it doesn't show signs of infidelity, then I think you're in a perfect relationship. But you still have to check her phone from time to time. Not because you think something is wrong, but just to know that you are paying attention to what she is doing on the phone.

Maybe I'm a little more tyrannical, but I think the woman needs to know that you can always check her phone if you want. After all, if she respects you, she won't have things on the phone that will bother you.

That doesn't mean she won't cheat on you. If she wants to do it, she will cheat on you even if she doesn't have a phone at all.

And if you are afraid of being considered jealous, then I only tell you this: jealousy is that fear of losing the person next to you. What you do is not out of fear. You just want to make sure she's loyal to you. If you find it isn't, then show her the door, and you're done.

Do you know the difference between a jealous man and one who is not jealous? When something is wrong, a real man will say goodbye to the wrong partner. A jealous man will scream, threaten, resort to physical acts, do many vile things but will never say goodbye because the biggest fear for him is the fear of abandonment.

## 4. Can a woman change, or if she cheated on you once, she would always cheat?

My answer is as simple as it is sharp: I don't know, and I don't care. And not because I would be ignorant, but because I can't afford to take risks. I'm not willing to pawn my future and give someone a second chance.

I'm not a psychologist to tell you if a woman can change, I'm not a sociologist to know how she will behave after she cheated on you so that you won't find a well-documented answer here.

Realistically speaking, we should all learn from our mistakes. I'm sure there are women who, after cheating, realized they were wrong and never made that mistake again. How many women are in this situation? I have no way of knowing. And I don't think it's relevant.

Because you're not very interested in statistics, you didn't buy the book to find a number. You came in to find out if your wife or girlfriend will cheat on you again, in case you forgive her. And no one knows the answer to your question.

Only you will be able to find the answer to this question if you take the risk. But the stakes are too high for me, and I could never risk so much. I prefer to start a new game and start my life over, at the risk of not finding what I want and not finding the happiness I am looking for.

Because the moment you decide to forgive her, you bet all your happiness and all your future on the idea that she will never cheat on you again. And there will be women who will cheat, there will be women who will not cheat. But what do you do if she is among those who will repeat the mistake?

Are you willing to waste a few years of your life finding out the answer to your question? Are you willing to put your happiness at stake for this?

You know very well what advice I give you when you are deceived, leave and not look back. But I also understand those who give their wives a second chance. I don't support them, but I understand them.

My only problem is another. The decision must be made. No matter what you decide is, the only culprit for the outcome is you.

If you find out over the years that she hasn't changed and learned nothing from the chance you gave her, you'll find the culprit in the mirror. It's not her, it's not her mother, it's not God, it's you. Because we are no longer children, and your actions have consequences.

I could never take such a risk, so I will never know on my own if a woman who cheated on me is capable of change. I don't get a second life; I don't have years or decades to waste finding the answer to this question.

And in the end, in years to come, you will see that you asked the wrong question. Instead of wondering if she would cheat on you again, you had to wonder if you could be happy with her again. Because in vain did she remain faithful to you if the relationship was destroyed by mistrust and jealousy.

## 5. Do you think she's going to the gym for you?

Many men are taken by surprise by a breakup. We ignore the signs of a relationship ending and wake up shocked when confronted with the accomplished fact. Today we are learning a sign of a relationship that is coming to an end.

When a man interacts with a woman, physical appearance matters the most. Until you discover her personality, sense of humour, or intelligence, you see her body. And women know that. And she also knows that a body without extra pounds will attract a man's eyes much better. Which man? Let's see.

It's great for your body to be in shape. It is perfect for keeping clean and going to the gym regularly. It's good for your health, and no one can deny it. But that's not why we're going to the gym. Most people go to the gym to catch the eye of others. And this is true for both men and women.

Yes, health is good, but we men go to the gym to look good, to be liked by women. When we make six-packs, we also do it for women. I'm not a fitness expert, but I don't think those who struggle to make six-packs make all that effort for health reasons. The same goes for women. They go to the gym and train, mainly to be attractive to us.

If your wife has been going to the gym since you know her and has been on a regular diet, then most likely this is her lifestyle, she's not doing it for someone, in particular, she's doing it for her.

Suppose she is not passionate about healthy living but has recently started going to the gym and taking care of herself. In that case, she wants to become more attractive. For you, for someone else in particular, or men in general.

And how do you know who is she going for at the gym? It's simple. You look at her actions. Do you see her trying to conquer you, or do you feel more and more distant? Is she still making time for you? Do you see her dress provocatively when she's with you, or just when she leaves home alone? All you have to do is always ask who she's trying to attract.

Sex is the best indicator of a relationship. If everything is like the beginning of the relationship, do not worry, she is trying to lose weight for you.

If sexually, the relationship is not the same as in the beginning, but you see her trying, you see her initiating intimate relationships as often as possible, you see that she wants to spend time with you, then be sure that for you she is trying to lose weight. She probably thinks she's not attractive enough to you anymore, and she's trying to do something about it.

But if you notice that she has started going to the gym, she has started to take care of herself, but she still can't find time for you to go for a walk together, she is not trying to become attractive for you.

If she suddenly became interested in the way she looks, but when you try to initiate physical contact, she constantly refuses you, again she is not trying to become attractive for you.

And yet, for whom does she want to become attractive? Since her attraction to you has disappeared, she may be attracted to another man she is trying to conquer, and her physical appearance plays a vital role.

That doesn't necessarily mean he's cheating on you. It just means that she has mentally left the relationship and is preparing for the next one. She may try to become attractive to men in general, knowing that it will be easy for her to find someone after breaking up with you.

Whatever your reasons, you should be prepared to hear the old phrase "we must talk."

## 6. She cheated on you, but are you convinced it was something strictly sexual for her?

Let's take a look at the situation. You are her husband. You should be the one who excites her so much that she has no eyes for another. And yet, it's not like that.

What does this situation tell me about you? That you don't attract her. I can tell you that sexually, you're not the man she wants. That you don't meet her needs as a woman.

If you are talking about reconciliation, you may be very good at bringing resources home. But that woman feels very little satisfaction when she chooses to marry you. She feels that she has chosen the safe path, not the best path.

You see, a woman's DNA knows two types of men. The Alpha male, the one who sexually attracts her and has good genes, and the Beta male, the one who does not have an extraordinary genetic material but can gather resources and help her raise a child.

Which archetype do you think you belong to? And if you're not sure, let me tell you straight. The fact that it was just sex, she didn't have feelings, means that this guy is Alpha. It means that the other guy is a real man, and this guy will always attract her.

And why did it happen? Because you're not that type of man. You likely have a good job, and you will be able to help her raise a child, but she does not want your genetic material. Or maybe you didn't know how to treat her like a sexual being. Whatever the reason, she's attracted to real men, and you weren't one.

So, if you were glad that she didn't put feelings in the extramarital affair, find out from me that she just told you that you're not her kind of man. She will stay with you as long as you can bring resources, but sexually, you are not her first choice.

And I want to be very well understood. I'm not speaking badly of her here. Okay, she doesn't give a damn about loyalty, and you have to say goodbye instantly. But I understand it perfectly.

Because few men excite her, out of these, only a few also like her. And even fewer are single. And of these, there are very few who want to be in a relationship with her.

Why do I say that? Understand that it's hard for her to find the man of her dreams and so, she gets to know you.

You don't make her get wet instantly, but you're a good boy. You have a good job, and you don't lose your money at the casino. You also have some hobbies in common. You are also a smart boy, you can talk for hours together. You spend your evenings on TV, like an average couple. Boring, but normal. And you treat her very nicely, flowers, compliments, and declarations of love.

All good and beautiful until HE appears. Because there is always an HE. HE no longer has any of your qualities, and yet HE makes her think only of him. It makes her feel like a woman; it makes her feel as if she wants to be submissive and wants to be dominated by HIM as if she wants to be "taken" by HIM.

Her fault is that she is not loyal. Your fault is that you have the impression that she should have eyes only for you, as long as, instead of becoming like HIM, you indulge in your way of being. You want her to have eyes only for you as long as you don't even understand why HE excites her and you don't.

What makes you think that from now on, you will have more luck in interacting with women, as long as you do not know what they want and what kind of stimuli they respond to? What will happen when another HE appears in her life?

**7. Do you fully trust your wife? Do not overlook the signs of infidelity!**

I'm not telling you to be jealous here! Either way, jealousy is terrible. Jealousy does not let you sleep at night, making you live with an obsessive fear that your woman is not faithful to you.

First of all, your wife is not your wife because slavery has long been abolished. This desire to own your wife is a little sick, and you should talk to a psychologist. In time, you will come to terms with the idea that the woman is not yours, it's just your turn. Enjoy today.

Secondly, you cannot use jealousy to prevent possible infidelity. There is no point in forbidding them to go out for a drink with their girlfriends, or to stay overtime at work, or to talk to someone in particular. Why?

Because if a woman wants to cheat on you, she will cheat on you, and you have little to prevent. Okay, you can become the ideal man for her and be the most attractive man in her life. But even so, you can't be sure she won't cheat on you.

What can you do? You can come to terms with the thought that if she wants to cheat on you, any woman will cheat on you. You can gain confidence knowing that she is the one who loses in this case. You can see your life without being obsessed with what can happen. But you don't have to be stupid.

What do I mean by that? Don't make infidelity an obsession as long as you can't do much to prevent it, but don't shut yourself up in your world or start ignoring the signs of infidelity.

You can take care of how you choose your partner, you can take care to maintain the attraction between you, and you can develop as a man so much that it would be wrong to risk losing you.

Guess what? Even in this case, women will take risks for various reasons, too unimportant. The point is, if it's going to happen, it's going to happen, and there's no point in stressing it out. I mean, don't bother looking for signs of infidelity, but when they do, don't ignore them.

Because if you feel that something is wrong, then you will have to check it. The opposite of jealousy is not ignorance, it is self-confidence. The idea that you should give your wife blind trust is just ignorance. I know I'm radical now, but no one deserves blind trust, not even you.

You have to trust your wife, but when instinct tells you something is wrong, it's time to check what's going on. You can't live with the fear of being deceived, but it's also not good to live with your head in the ground, like an ostrich.

I'm not saying to confront her, make a fuss, or start giving her ultimatums. If, for example, you feel that she is getting colder with you and starts doing overtime at work, it's time to pay a little more attention to her behaviour.

You can start by listening very carefully to what she says about being overtime. Are there inconsistencies in what she says? If you feel she's not being honest, then that's a problem. Do you think the reason given is not extremely good? Check it out.

I don't know exactly your situation. Every person is different, and every relationship is different, but look for answers.

If you find out she's cheating on you, then it's simple. We would all like to believe that our wife would never do that, but sometimes life beats the movie. In that case, say goodbye. No explanations, no confrontations, no circus, and no dramas.

I don't think that's jealousy, as long as you don't do it for fear of losing her. I don't confuse the fear of losing her because no one deserves my complete trust.

Jealousy is just fear and insecurity. When your motives are not fear, I don't think it's jealousy.

You can't forbid a woman to go out for a drink with her friends. But suppose you know that those girlfriends negatively influence her. In that case, you can tell her that you don't want to be in a relationship with a woman who goes out drinking with those girlfriends.

She is free to do what she wants. On the other hand, you have to be willing to say goodbye if she goes for that juice. Simply because you don't want that kind of relationship. Are you jealous if you do that? No, you're just very clear on what you want.

**8. Do you want to forgive her for the sake of the child? You're making a mistake!**

Congratulations, you have just decided to traumatize your child and teach him how to have a shitty relationship with his future partner.

I am perfectly convinced that you are saying the eternal expression: a child needs both parents. And you're wrong. The child does not need the parents to be married. He needs both parents to get involved in his life. Your simple cohabitation does not bring any benefit to the child. On the contrary, if the relationship between the parents is not healthy, that is not a good enviroment to raising a child.

And yet, what does the child need? He needs people to play male and female roles in his life. Whether you have a son or a daughter, your child needs to learn how a woman behaves and how a man behaves.

If you can forgive your wife for infidelity, you have nothing to teach your child. Do you want to pass on to your child the idea that if his wife sleeps with another man, he has to accept it? Do you want to teach your daughter that it is okay to cheat on her husband because there are no consequences?

And jealousy? That jealousy of you grinds every time you're not sure what your wife is doing. Is that what you want to teach your child? An embarrassing excuse for a man arguing with his wife for looking more than two seconds into a man's eyes on the street?

Because yes, you will become that man. You will be intimidated by any stranger on the street passing by. You just don't think you're going to trust her. You already know how much you can trust her.

And it's not like you're confident enough to be jealous. What confidence do you have in yourself? Well, are you a man? You don't think that out of 3.5 billion women, you will find one who deserves your trust, so you forgive your wife and put all the responsibility on the little one. So if you're going to have a shitty life, you're not to blame, you're just trying to do what's best for your little one.

How heroic of you, how you sacrificed your life for a higher cause, for the good of your descendants. As a weak man, you are willing to forgive her moments of sex with another man. Forgive, not forget, because you will not be able to sleep for nights thinking about your wife in your lover's arms.

Twenty years from now, when your son will look at you and see how many regrets you have in life, how many grievances when he will think that you have been in that relationship for his good, he will do nothing but blame himself for his unhappiness. When sleepless nights, quarrels out of jealousy, and insecurity cut wrinkles on your eternally frowning face, the child will see them and feel responsible for them.

Have you ever noticed how couples who say they stayed together for the child's good do not divorce in the second after the child moves out of the house? Or if they divorce, the one who asks for the divorce is also the one who cheated, not the one who forgave? I'm wondering why?

Because the idea that you forgave her for the good of the child is just a lie that you tell the world because it sounds so much better than "I'm a weak man, and I'm willing to accept shit only not to be alone."

If you want to forgive her, forgive her. But don't lie to your child.

If you want to forgive her, forgive her because you love her, because you want to see if there are any chances to return to normal, forgive her because you may not have also been faithful. Forgive her because you still believe in her, forgive her because you are stupid, forgive her because you are weak, but do not involve your child in your wrong decisions.

And something else. I know you do this because you don't want to suffer. You are aware that there would be much suffering in your life, and I do not contradict you, it is tough to get a divorce. But what no one is telling you is that you have decided to take your suffering in instalments.

That is, instead of saying stop and start over, followed by one, two, sometimes even three years of suffering, you decide to divide your suffering into instalments over several years. Many years in which you will not have a healthy relationship. Many years crushed by jealousy, uncertainty, the fear of losing it again. Many years in which the psyche knows that you have decided not to respect yourself.

## 9. In fact, your wife does not regret that she cheated on you!

Are you sure your wife regrets the infidelity? So, what if she regrets it? I guarantee she'll do it again. Shee will deceive you again and regret it again. Why? Because you deserve. Because instead of being a man, you are weak.

Let's get along. She's not sorry she did it, she's sorry you found out. If you are lucky, she regrets that you found out, and your relationship suffers because of it. I say you're lucky because that indicates that mentally she hasn't left the relationship yet, or she hasn't left it entirely, and she still wants to be with you.

How romantic does that sound? My wife slept with someone else, but she still wants to be with me. Isn't it cool how love always wins? I hope you realized how stupid it sounds.

Now let me explain the uglier part. She has no regrets that she cheated on you. That cheating was not a 5-minute interaction that she could not control, and she woke up in the unpleasant situation in which a stranger had sex with her while she was thinking about you and the love between you.

Her extramarital affair was an assumed, conscious decision, and she even wanted to cheat. Otherwise, she was filing a rape complaint.

And yes, some women regret the extramarital affair. Some regret that they cheated because the experience was not as pleasant as they hoped. Or there were very few benefits and too many inconveniences.

There are also women whose conscience does not give them peace because they sincerely regret what they did. Those women are worthy of almost all respect. And I say almost all the respect because no matter how much they regret it today, they did what they did. It's like a court. If you admit the deed and regret it, you will receive a lesser punishment, but you will not escape the punishment.

Even if this is the best situation, you will still have to divorce. First of all, your wife doesn't love you anymore. Or she no longer loves you the way you want. If you don't believe me, I remind you that she slept with another man. Wow, she loves you so much, wake up.

Secondly, she regrets what she did today, which does not guarantee that it will not be repeated. And I wish you success in gaining confidence in her again.

Third, she didn't mislead you about your relationship with her. She never said, "Lord, what a wonderful husband I have and what a beautiful life I lead, let me go and sleep with another man." You're to blame, too. Simply put, you have to develop as a human being.

If you try to become the best version of yourself but do not dare to divorce a wife who cheated on you, you will fail.

And last but not least, my old problem, you are not a man! A real man loves and respects himself so much that he cannot forgive his wife for infidelity. When you don't get the respect you deserve, you leave. Why are you staying?


## 10. Forgive her infidelity! But don't forget.

Before you go out that door, forgive her! But don't forget to go out the door!

In addition to the feeling that you are Jesus Christ who has just forgiven someone's sins, it will help you heal faster. You gain nothing if you complain, just as you gain nothing if you ask her for explanations.

She did it, what does it matter? She did it. After all, She's immature. She doesn't value loyalty because she didn't love you enough.

You are in a situation where you are going to make a series of mistakes. Starting with the way you chose the person with whom to enter into a relationship, continuing with the systematic way of not taking into account the negative signals you saw in her, and ending with your behaviour in the relationship with her.

And yes, you did not behave appropriately in the relationship. Why? Because even an immature woman, who does not give a damn about loyalty, will be faithful to you as long as you do the right thing in the relationship and she is entirely in love with you. Here I am not saying to overwhelm her with gifts, poems, and serenades. It means you weren't a real man, and you didn't let her be a woman.

You don't have to tell her that you forgive her, you don't owe her anything, you just have to find peace of mind when you leave your former marital home. Know that it is just a step in your life, which allows you to discover your mistakes and learn from them. A step that will be difficult, but from moments like this, we learn, these moments shape us as people.

Mistakes pay off, and you now pay for your mistakes, but if you don't learn from them, you'll repeat them and end up paying for them again. Even if the only thing you learn from your divorce is how to choose the woman with whom to enter into a relationship, you have an excellent chance of never experiencing the suffering caused by infidelity.

Suppose you also learn how to behave in a relationship. In that case, you have a good chance of having a functional relationship to be happy.

What I'm trying to tell you here is that this period is about learning, about development. It's not about pointing the finger and blaming others.

And if you feel you can't forgive her, then don't forgive her, but tell me later if all that hatred helps you with anything.

Or maybe you want to end up hating all women for what your ex did to you, maybe you want to be left with emotional scars and not be able to have a normal relationship with the next woman in your life because your ex-wife did what she did. Sounds like a good plan!

Maybe you are satisfied with the status of a man who no longer trusts women, but I assure you that you will have relationships with women in your life. And what are you going to do then? You will have a dysfunctional relationship because you cannot trust your life partner.

And after you've forgiven her, make sure you don't forget what happened to you. Never forget what happened to you! Learn all you can from what happened. Analyze the former relationship and see what signals your ex-wife gave you, and you ignored them. Analyze her behaviour and what your behaviour led to infidelity.

And don't forget anything. Because life is long and you may reencounter the same situation. And if you make the same mistake twice, then it's just your fault.


**11. Will you ever be able to trust a woman again?**

Suppose you blindly believed in your ex-wife, and your expectations were deceived, then today. In that case, you are undoubtedly reluctant to trust another woman. How long does this mistrust last? Until you become wiser.

It lasts until the day you come to truly accept what happened to you, the day you accept that the same thing may happen to you again, and the day you look at yourself, and you will recognize that if you suffer again, you will not die, it is not the end of the road, you will only take it once again from the beginning.

This will be one of the most beautiful days of your life, the day when you realize that divorce did not bring you down, that it was difficult for you, not impossible. The day you declare yourself a winner when you will not be afraid of another divorce because you know that you are stronger than him.

Typically, it's tough to trust a woman if you've been cheated on, but that's not life either. I don't think your childhood dream was to be left alone forever because a woman cheated on your confidence at the age of 30. You can't always be afraid of being cheated on again or turn your life into a bad spy movie where you keep trying to see what the other person is doing.

And do you know what I think? I think there are women among us who deserve all our respect and all our trust. Women who will receive your trust and turn it into something extraordinary. But do you know what their flaw is? They look exactly like the ones that, at some point, will end up cheating on you.

I hope I'm wrong, I hope to discover the magic formula, but at least today, I don't think you can tell reliable women from those who in a year, two, ten will make you regret believing in them. I think some signs disqualify some of them, but I am convinced that there are women who will not give you any signs before they deceive you, just as there are women who would never deceive your trust.

And since the solution is not to become paranoid and stay on your toes for the next 40 years, you best wake up. What does this mean? Learn to pay attention and avoid dysfunctional behaviour when choosing your partner; you will have to give her the confidence she expects once you have chosen her.

And yet, does the woman next to you deserve your absolute trust? I do not think so! In fact, in the beginning, no one deserves your trust, just as you will not deserve her trust! But you will grant it. Yes, you should do it for yourself, not for her, because it's awful to sit at 10 in the evening wondering if she's actually gone to bed or just going to the club with her friends.

And I'm sorry to let you know that it's possible to give your trust to someone who doesn't deserve it, but the divorce you're going through also has some advantages. For example, today, I am over 30 years old, and I feel that in the end, I think with my brain and not with other parts of the body. Although the desire is often remarkable, the brain can stop when it feels that something is wrong.

Divorce has its advantages, you will learn at what to pay attention to a woman before and after you have given her your trust. And because there are so many criteria to consider, I will not detail them here, I will give just one example: self-esteem, you must learn to respect yourself. What does this have to do with the trust placed in her?

A woman, even one who does not give a damn about loyalty, will not cheat on her husband if she respects him. You must respect yourself. So it will be harder to fool you.

And the best part is just coming. By respecting yourself, you will feel when she no longer treats you with respect, and then you will decide for yourself if you break up with her (because I don't see the reason for a relationship with someone who no longer respects you), or you somehow regain her respect.

Either way, if she passes your tests, give her all your confidence because I assure you that if something terrible happens, you will see so many signs that you will certainly not be taken by surprise as the first time. And anyway, you have no choice!


## 12. Your wife cheated on you. What do you do next?

Say goodbye! Simple! That's about it, but unfortunately, it's not enough for some of you. No matter how hard it is for you, no matter how hard you think it will be for you from today onwards, you have no way back. You just can't stay with it and keep your dignity.

Stop rationalizing her actions and wondering why it happened. All that matters is that it happened. You have to understand that it will happen again. Any mistake that does not produce repercussions will be repeated.

No matter what reason she gives you, your wife simply loves you so much and respects you so much that she couldn't help but have sex with someone else. I know I'm cruel, I know it's not what you want to hear, but life is hard, and she doesn't care that you're a sensitive soul who can't stand the truth and wants to continue believing in fairy tales.

One of the worst ideas in this world is to ask women for advice about other women. It's a lot to explain, but in short, women don't know exactly what they want or don't want to tell you because they don't want to hurt you. Instead, most women you ask will tell you that the man who forgives his wife after infidelity is not respected and is not a man.

You simply have no excuse to forgive her, you are weak, and that's what all women, including your wife, know. Suppose you keep talking to other women about relationships. In that case, they may tell you another universally valid truth: women cheat differently from men.

If a man cheats, it does not mean that he no longer loves his wife. He may love her, but something is missing in their relationship. Instead, when a woman cheats, she no longer loves her husband but also disrespects him for whatever reason.

A woman cheats when she is emotionally detached from her husband.

Can you ever trust her again? Can you still sit quietly at home, not knowing exactly what she is doing at the moment? Can you rest easy if she stays overtime one night? Can you ever sit still while she is away on a delegation or out with her friends in the city?

Simply put, will you be able to stay calm as long as you don't know what she's doing 24 hours a day? Will you be able to rest easy when you see that she is receiving messages and you do not know from whom? But when she talks on the phone to a stranger, can you keep calm? Suppose you have to leave the city for a week in the interest of work. Will you be able to leave without feeling heartbroken, knowing that you are leaving her alone at home and it can happen again?

Do you remember how hopeful and in love you were at the beginning of the relationship? Is that what you dreamed of becoming your relationship? Was that your dream? Staying in the house with someone you can't trust? You can't look into her eyes without imagining the moments when she was having sex with someone behind your back?

Before you met her, when you were thinking about what the perfect woman should look like in your vision, did you ever say you wanted a woman to cheat on you?

I know you'll be tempted to get it back, and I know why. Your phrase "I don't want to lose her" translates to "I know she's not the kind of woman I want, but I can't find a better one." And guess what? You are perfectly right!

Today, I have to convince you that you are a weak man if you get her back. We get what we deserve from life. If we are happy with little, we will receive little. On the other hand, if we are not happy with little and fight for something better, we will receive something better.

Quality women want quality men, and you are not one of them. A strong man would have said goodbye from the second he discovered infidelity.

You have to understand that the humiliation you alone endure can be seen on your face, you can't hide it. Do you know what is one of the main traits that a woman is attracted to a man? Self-confidence. What confidence do you think you have if you don't dare to say goodbye if you are not firmly convinced that you deserve it and you can find something better than it?

Do you think that in the morning, when you look in the mirror at the failure you have become, you will gain confidence? But when she didn't answer your message for an hour and a half? But when you look into the eyes of your friends who know you were deceived and yet forgave her? Do you think that you will feel strong? Do you think you're going to feel like a man? Will your parents be proud of you?

What kind of woman do you think will accept to have a relationship with a weak man like you? When she finds out that you forgave your ex for infidelity, will it seem like a good thing? Will she consider you the ideal man for her?

So you're right, you won't find a better one because you don't deserve it. If you want another better woman, you have to get better, and you have to start today, saying goodbye.

Yes, you will suffer, it will be hard for you. You will come home from work and find the house empty. The places where you went out together will cause you an oppressive sadness. You will feel that a part of you is missing, and it will be damn hard for you to start over.

But guess what? The weak will give up, the weak will humble themselves, the weak will give up the fight, but the difference is made between the first place and second place. Women want to be winners, not participants. Nobody cares about second place or third place.

I can't promise you that you will find a better woman than her, it just depends on you and how much you are willing to do to become a better version of yourself, but I can promise you that you will get out of this relationship with head up, respecting yourself. The others will respect you because, in the end, you will respect yourself.

The irony of fate is that your ex-wife will start respecting you again because she knows it takes a man for a decision like this. The ultimate irony of fate is that she will be attracted to you again, but don't give up hope, if you give in to her advances, you will show her that you are not strong and will return to today's stage. Correct: the real irony of fate is that her infidelity can become the best thing that ever happened to you.

If you will use this suffering to open your eyes and see the world as it is, if you learn how to be a man if you learn to value yourself, always to put yourself first, to develop as a human being, if you will learn what women want from a man to have a happy relationship with the next woman in your life, then your ex-wife is the one who triggered your personal development.

You will come in a year to realize that without knowing her, you would not have gotten where you got, and if you had not been wrong, you would not have changed anything about yourself. So accept that some people come into our lives just to give us some lessons and help us grow, accept that your ex-wife gave you one of the most important lessons, that you have to be a man.

Try to break up with her just by being grateful for everything she did for you. After a while, when you will be happy in another relationship, you will have to admit that it is also her merit.

# III. BE A MAN!

## 1. Parting day. We have to talk!

It's over. Three ruthless yet straightforward words have just trampled on your illusion of happy family life: we need to talk.

Please don't be silly, it's not a negotiation. It's a notification. You are being informed of a decision already made by her, and it is not much you can do.

Mentally, your wife was long gone, physically a few more formalities were needed. The first formality is your notification.

Don't be fooled that there should be a dialogue. It doesn't matter. The reasons do not change the fact that you will be left alone. You will not be "less divorced" because ……. (enter shitty reason here)…...

Your part of the conversation is simple: "It's not what I want. If you change your mind, you can call me. " That's all you have to say. Any extra word is useless and tarnishes your image as a man capable of overcoming a difficult situation.

Today it is not about personal development, it is about suffering. Quickly and politely end the conversation with her and go somewhere alone with your thoughts, and cry. Yes, cry! You have nothing better to do today!

As long as you are the only being in the universe who will know you are crying, go and cry! It will be much easier for you after you start to recover if you do not keep this suffering accumulated in you.

Regardless of your emotional discharge method (crying, shooting with a gun in the polygon, the boxing bag at the gym), do it so that no one sees this side of you. Don't beg for mercy. Maybe you feel that it helps you at the moment, but you will have to feel that you are a strong man to go everywhere in the long run. So keep your image strong, (what's left of it), and suffer in silence.

Don't ask too many questions today. Today is about acceptance. Accept what is happening to you, and your healing will be more effortless. We'll take care of your problems later.

## 2. Stop negotiating at departure, you have nothing to sell!

Many men start negotiating on the day of parting: „I can change, you will see! I'll be the man you want. Are you saying I didn't pay enough attention to you? From today, my universe will revolve around you. You know that thing you don't like about me? I will become another man! I already feel like another man! All you have to do is love me!"

Bend down a little to raise your dignity from the ground, where you let it fall, and sprint to the bathroom where you can look in the mirror to see a fool!

You're the one who sells Christmas trees on December 28th. Nobody wants your goods anymore, nobody needs your goods anymore, but you insist. You don't want to understand that the woman in front of you doesn't want to buy anything, she just wants to refuse you nicely.

If I think about it, I was wrong. You have something to sell! Do you know that strong, self-controlled man she fell in love with many years ago? That image is all you can sell, although today, that strong man is full of mistrust, he is insecure about himself, needs constant validation from his wife and friends, and blames anyone other than him for this mess.

Show her that man is still alive, be a man and accept the situation without negotiating, without humiliating yourself, without compromising.

We, as men, have always wondered what women want, and we have never come to a standard answer. Although I will detail later, I will now tell you what women want: women want men! When I say they want men, I don't mean penis wearers, I mean they want men and not boys.

They want men to behave like men so that they can be feminine. In addition to masculine physical traits, she wants to see masculine behavior traits. Do you know what a man does when a woman abandons him? Accept the situation and move on. Are you a man?


## 3. Why is your ex-wife still looking for you?

Although she has been away from home for some time, she wants you to remain friends. She is very interested in helping you get through these difficult moments, and she wants to know that you are well. You may not realize it, but the sooner you break the connection, the healing will begin.

Most of the time, you hurt yourself with your ideas and facts. You have the idea that if you keep in touch, you will somehow find a middle ground and come to terms. She may be right when she tells you that she only needs a little space to think and put her life in order. You have to show her that you love her and wait for her to decide what she wants, and you will be together.

Or maybe she doesn't even realize what a good boy she lost. You lie to yourself.

No matter what reasons you find for keeping in touch, she has only two reasons why she does it, and neither of them is acceptable for a man.

If she is no longer attracted to you, she keeps in touch just because she feels sorry for you. She doesn't want you to remain friends; she just wants to know that you managed to get over the divorce. As time goes on and you are more and more reconciled with the idea of divorce, you will notice that you will communicate less and less until the point where the contact will disappear completely.

In this case, you were just a "mom's boy" who needs babysitting and is not considered strong enough to get over the shock of a divorce. Either way, she doesn't think you're pretty manly.

If there is a minimal attraction left for you, she will try to keep you as a backup. she will be satisfied with you too, but only after she has enjoyed everything that life gets in her way. Don't get me wrong: she will go out to the club, she will go out with various individuals, she will come home with some of them, she will try to find you a replacement.

After a while, when her biological clock will beat harder and harder and still not be able to find someone better, you will be "good enough". How can you, as a man, know that you are good enough for your wife? You're not what she wanted to be, but she didn't find anyone better than you. No matter how you say it, if you agree to come back to your wife, you are a disgrace to masculinity.

Don't get me wrong, it's not the easiest thing to do. The most painful thing about a breakup is ending the contract.

Please take a look around you, you may know a guy who, after being abandoned by his girlfriend or wife, is still in touch with her and is now friends. Do you think that guy is a real man?

In a moment of sincerity, any woman will recognize that such a guy is not a man and could not always respect him because he does not respect himself. The moment you stop any contact, you show her that you are a man. You show her that you respect yourself enough not to accept half measures, and at the same time, you are strong enough to get over it.

Two qualities will certainly not go unnoticed, provided that she has a minimum of attraction to you.

You may not know it yet, but respect is essential in a relationship. A woman cannot love a man she does not respect and will not respect him forever if she does not respect himself. If you were to look back, you'd see that respect disappeared first in your relationship, and here's your fault.

So, from today, you will have to start respecting yourself. I know it's hard, that's why not everyone does it.

## 4. How do you behave with your child's mother?

Simple, keep in touch as little as possible and as professional as possible.

When you call someone interested in work, you are elegant, respectful, short, and to the point. You don't talk about your personal life, nor do you prolong the conversation longer than necessary. Call, set up business details, and close respectfully.

The conversation doesn't have to last long, you don't have to be interested in her personal life, and you have to be the one to end the conversation. If she asks you personal questions, try to divert the discussion to the child.

Don't try to show her how well you're doing after the breakup because you're embarrassing yourself and nobody believes you. If you want to show her that you're fine without her when you meet her, show a small smile, a face of a man who doesn't look like he's been crying all night after her, and a total lack of interest in her.

In business, the supplier is important. A good relationship with the supplier is ideal, but it is not essential because the supplier is not irreplaceable. We can always find another supplier, even if it means higher purchase prices or shortages in supply for a while.

But at the same time, the provider needs us to survive. It is a simple negotiation in which we have a slight advantage.

Coming back to our problem, your wife is a provider. It can give you free access to the child, or you can go to court and receive the right to visit. She has to gain from a good relationship with you because she also needs you to raise your child or simply because she understands that a child also needs a father.

What do I want you to understand from here? A good relationship with the former is significant, but it is not essential. If she has some absurd requirements or you do not feel treated with respect, get up from the negotiating table and go to court to see your child.

Don't be naive, this is a negotiation. The way you present yourself at the negotiation is how you will be treated in the long run. If you look like a weak man, willing to compromise to see your children, you will pay for it.

In the real world, if you are weak, you are trampled on. And it's normal to be like that. Weak people have to be trampled on, it's been happening since the world, it's called natural selection, and that's how we make sure we perpetuate only the best genes.

If you are a man, you will say clearly what you want, namely to visit the child. Suppose the ex-wife starts to impose unacceptable conditions for a man. In that case, you get up from the negotiating table and go to court.

Yes, it is difficult to do this, you must be aware that you will not see your child for a while, but it is necessary. If you want to be a man, then be a man and do not accept filth. The men are mentally strong and hold out for a while until the court decides. If you accept absurd conditions today, then you will have to accept them for life.

As for the well-being of the child, yes, the child needs both parents. But do you know what else the child needs? A strong male example. If you are a weak man, without a spine, willing to compromise, and who does not respect himself at all, do you think that your son will ever become a strong man?

Do you think your daughter will ever learn to respect a man and have a healthy relationship with a man? Or do you think she'll act exactly like your ex-wife and treat men like garbage? Do you think that your daughter will look for healthy relationships with strong men or will look for relationships with weak men, easy to manipulate?

Children will always do what they see at home, so take a good look in the mirror and think that what you see in the mirror now is what your son will become over the years, and such a partner will look for your daughter for a relationship. Is that what you want for them?

Your child needs to see healthy relationships, both between parents and in your future relationships. If you are rebuilding your life after divorce, the little one must see that you have a functional relationship. He will learn from your relationship and later imitate it when he enters your relationship.

Suppose your child comes every two weeks to stay with you. In that case, he must see that you have a healthy relationship with a woman, to see how two people behave in a couple, what is love and what is the respect between two people. Boy or girl, your child will learn from you what it means to be a man. Are you proud of what you teach your child?

## 5. Why do women get over separation faster?

Although it's only been a few days since she left you, your ex is already seeing someone else. You still haven't had a good night's sleep without waking up in the middle of the night to think about it. You still can't function normally as a single man, and you see that she's already moving on.

Emotionally, you two are in different stages. If you looked coldly at the relationship that had just ended, you would notice that she had distanced herself for a long time, she was losing less and less interest, while you were probably trying to make her happy. You will find out later why this was a mistake on your part, but until then, you have to admit that in the end, you were alone in the relationship.

And yet, how can she already go out with someone else? Simple! Because she stayed with you until she didn't love you at all. Your ex did not leave you when she left home, your ex left you months ago but stayed with you until she found a replacement.

If you make big mistakes in the relationship or have behavioral issues, she will leave you directly. But if you make her lose her temper just because you're a weak man, then she'll only leave after she finds a replacement.

You are often the typical "nice guy", good boy, caring with her, you do all her whims, you love her incredibly much, and you would do anything for her. You often give up your needs to meet her needs and desires.

Don't be fooled, we didn't praise you! This attitude led you to divorce because, sexually, women are not attracted to men like this. She often knows you're a great guy and have a wonderful soul, but as long as it's not sexual attraction, you're just a good friend.

She has no tangible reason to leave you. She loves you like a brother, although it's not the thing she wanted when you met and had sex three times a day.

What happens when you no longer love your husband or wife? You start to look around, you start to develop emotional connections with other people, which may or may not lead to extramarital relationships.

Your wife was already looking elsewhere for what you had offered her at the beginning of the relationship. When you probably weren't so attached to her. When your universe worked without it. When you had other interests in life besides her well-being. When you could work without validating it. When you had a purpose and a plan for fighting.

Or maybe your wife is just looking for someone to seduce her sexually. Maybe she misses that crazy sex you miss too.

But even though you are suffering today and feel down to earth, your ex-wife is full of confidence because her plans are focused on your replacement. She is full of hope, she had probably rediscovered what sexual attraction is and relives what she felt with you when you met. Do you remember how you felt at first, in the first month? That's how she feels now, but with someone else.

Is she to blame here? Because it's easy to say she has questionable morals. It's easy to catalog it, it's easy to retake refuge under the victim's umbrella. It's easy to think you have no one to blame but guess what? That's how women are, and men probably do the same. You need to know that if you don't learn anything, history will most likely repeat itself.

You see, attraction is not easy to measure. And it's hard to explain. Women don't know very well why they are no longer attracted to you. They just feel that they are no longer attracted to you.

That's why, most of the time, the reasons you receive for parting are childish or irrational. Because she doesn't know exactly why she's breaking up with you either, and when she knows, she doesn't want to hurt you. No woman who still has an ounce of respect for you will tell you that you are not a man.

Why do I say it's your fault? Do you know who doesn't have these things? Do you know who is never abandoned because his wife no longer loves him? A man who can read his wife's level of attraction, a man who knows how sex attraction works, and a man who understands what women want. If you were that man, she wouldn't leave you!

We all laughed at jokes on the internet about the fact that it's impossible to understand women. We all liked the picture at least once in our lives with a 5000-page book that says "How to understand women, volume I". We all laughed at jokes like this because we have the impression that women are hard to understand.

Women are not difficult to understand at all, and you do not need to free your library to make room for the books you will learn to understand.

On the contrary, if you were, to be honest with yourself, you know someone who changes women weekly. You don't understand that maybe he doesn't know how women work either, but he knows completely what it means to be a man, and women respond to that.

If you think about it, the guy has very masculine features. Am I right that you don't dare to take him on? Am I right that he would stand up straight in front of you if you tried to humiliate him? Do you still think it's a coincidence that women constantly surround such men?

I know you are down to earth now, and you would rather have someone to comfort you, to tell you that you did not do anything wrong and the world is like in the fairy tale you believed in until now. Unfortunately, if I do that, you will enter into a new relationship and suffer the same thing.

But do you know anything? I promise you that if you get up from where you are now, and you learn what is needed to be learned, not only will you never be taken by surprise by a divorce, but you will know how to have a proper relationship with a woman. And most importantly, you will know how to ask exactly what you want from a woman.

Please don't lie to yourself; I know you didn't dare to tell her exactly what you wanted from her. Life is hard but simple when you know the rules. Don't you want to learn the rules?

## 6. After separation, get rid of her things quickly!

Today we clean. You don't need to remember her every time you open the closet. You don't need a degree in psychology to realize that it's a bad idea to think about it every 5 minutes.

I know you don't want to, I know it seems like there's still a chance she'll come back, but the reality is it's over, and you have to accept that.

At some point, you will have to get rid of those things. Wouldn't you like to get rid of them today, so that tomorrow you won't remember the past for everything you see in the house? Yes, it is a difficult step, but you know that I am right.

Pack everything that belongs to her and store them somewhere until she asks for her things. Don't try to use this pretext to contact her. If she wanted them, they would have been taken a long time ago, or she would have asked for them already.

You may think that if you haven't talked to her for a long time, the moment you contact her to solve the problem of the things left at home, you will open a way of communication that will lead to reconciliation. Unfortunately for you, life is not a Hollywood movie, and if she wanted to talk to you, she would have talked to you already.

So pack everything very nicely and with a lot of consideration, put her things in a storage room or a garage, and give her time to ask for them. Remember that you have to remain a gentleman and treat her things with respect you would treat something that is yours, not because you want to prove something to her, remember you are a gentleman.

Things that are yours but remind you of your EX must end up in the trash. If you want to get over a divorce, it's time to start a new life.

Yes, today is a sad day, you will feel like at a funeral because you will come to realize that it is over and there is no way back.

Take as much time as you think you need to do this, but do it, and don't leave any scraps to cling later when it's hard for you. All I can tell you is that it will be easier for you to get over if you clean today instead of postponing tomorrow.

Everything I told you today, I learned from my mistakes. I did not do what I wrote above. And I regretted it. I regretted it a lot. Don't be as stupid as me.

## 7. Women are neither bad nor good, women are women

You haven't reached this age without knowing that type of man who ends up saying the famous expression "all women are whores" after being cheated or abandoned. He is not sure if the earth is flat or not, but he knows clearly that "all women only look for money."

What's the matter here? Well, „Mike" didn't know all the women. Maybe some women are whores, maybe some are not. „Mike" was just hurt by a woman and vented his frustration on the rest of the women.

The problem is, „Mike" will get tired of being alone at some point, he'll try to find someone, and he won't know why no one wants to be with him.

The truth is, this hatred is felt. If you end up hating women, all you have to do is drive them away. Are women prostitutes? Probably yes, probably not. It matters a lot how you define the word. But I assure you that they are not all the same and if you know what to look for and what to pay attention to, you will find a quality woman.

After a divorce, many men discover that their wife is not who they thought she was. Immediately after, we discover character traits that we did not know, often the woman we break up with has nothing in common with the woman we married. And I don't know how to do it, but the qualities we discover in the former partner are never flattering.

But after analyzing my situation, I discovered one thing: those character traits had been there for a long time, but I overlooked them. I always had minor question marks, but I never gave them importance. I never knew how to connect several points to create a complete drawing.

I did not know, for example, that if a woman comes from a broken family, she will not know how to support a close-knit family. I never realized that if her mother doesn't respect her husband, she won't know how to respect her. My luck is that I have never met such women, but I am convinced that ten years ago, I would have closed my eyes to these little "details".

And I understand, „Mike" doesn't just see those character traits in his ex-wife. Mike sees a lot of women around him that he disagrees with. But „Mike" is stupid, or rather, „Mike" is misinformed. Mike has been lied to by the media, other women, or even lied to himself, believing that women should be in a certain way, and now he discovers that women are not what he thought they were.

I'm sorry, „Mike", but women don't stay virgins until you come on a white horse, and they don't refuse BMW owners because they prefer to live off your unemployment benefits. I'm sorry that real life is not what you dreamed of, but the solution is not to catalog women. The solution is to understand what is going on around you.

And yes, most women indeed turn their heads to an expensive car. But try to understand why. When you are at a traffic light, look at the driver of an expensive car and the cyclist waiting next to him. Which one do you think is the winner in life? Which do you think is more determined, more focused on his plans and his career.

Which do you think will get through life no matter how many difficulties and obstacles you encounter? Who do you think has a better chance of becoming a leader? If the situation becomes difficult, who do you think will avoid shrugging and blaming fate and will fight to emerge victoriously.

„Mike", if you were a woman, you wouldn't even look at the cyclist, and from all the things I've told you, I didn't question how beautiful the car is, I just told you what the car says about the driver. Appearances may be wrong, but they probably aren't.

I know it sounds cruel, but women don't want cyclists. I know we've been lied to for years that love "happens", but it's not. Women want winners, they want to look at you with respect, they want to feel admiration for you. Rather than cataloging them, you'd better begin to understand what they want from you.

And so as not to fall into the other extreme, I want to clarify something: women are not amazing, are not princesses, and do not deserve respect just because they were born without the Y chromosome.

Many have undesirable character traits. Many have offensive behavior towards other people, many have childhood trauma or lack of education. Many have diagnosed or undiagnosed mental health problems. Many have grown up in a divided family and will end up making your life a living hell if you make a family with them.

BUT, the same can be said about men—word by word.

What to do? Open your eyes the next time you meet someone, learn what to look out for, and you will find quality women.


## 8. The best way to tell your EX everything you feel.

I don't know why the next exercise works, I just know it works. A psychologist will probably tell you exactly why the exercise is good, I only know that it worked for me, and I advise you to use it too. However, it is good to express yourself, to verbalize what you feel, what grinds you.

I'm sure you have a lot to blame your ex-wife, I'm sure you still have nights when you can't sleep trying to reconcile with what happened. The problem is that it will be difficult for you to see your life while it still hurts that your ex cheated on you, lied to you, humiliated you, or ….. (fill in the blank).....

If you're wasting your time thinking about how she could do something like this to you, you're not ready to go through a divorce. Opportunities pass you by every day, but you are stuck in the past. And I understand you because there are so many things you would like to say to her, but it doesn't make sense.

Why put your soul on the tray to someone who has left you? Did she ask you how you felt? Did she ask you if you were suffering? And if she asked you, do you think she cares? If she cared about you, she was with you. So take out a piece of paper and a pen because we're writing a letter today.

Dear ex-wife,….... And start writing. Say it all. Everything you wanted to tell her, everything you feel, everything that holds you in place. Everything you have kept in your mind lately must appear in black and white on that sheet. Everything you want to know about yourself and what happened between you. All the things you didn't dare to tell her while you were still together. All your mistakes and all her mistakes. All the bad decisions that brought you to this situation.

Or maybe you want to thank her for everything she did for you, good or bad, and the lessons learned from what happened. Whatever you want to tell her, it should appear on paper.

In the end, read it a few times to make sure everything is correct, and you haven't forgotten anything, and throw it away! Break it into small pieces and throw it away. You are the only person who should read that letter. If you go to a psychologist, you can show it to him, but otherwise, no one should see that letter. I want to emphasize how important it is for your ex-wife never to read the letter.

I know you've seen a lot of Hollywood movies where these romantic gestures lead to a happy ending, but your life is not a Hollywood movie. I know that such a letter seems a romantic gesture in movies, but it is a desperate gesture in everyday life. You will look desperate and compassionate, and there is nothing romantic about this.

Even if you don't try to reconcile with her, you want to tell her what you have in mind to reconcile more easily with the idea of divorce, you will still seem desperate and weak. Why? Because she didn't ask your opinion. No one asked you how you felt because she didn't care.

Think that someone is talking to you and telling you something, you tell him clearly that you don't care about his problem, but he keeps telling his problems. What did you think of that person? A good opinion? Well, you are that person when you keep in touch with someone who has left you.

The moment she left you, she considered herself superior to you. Why would you make a gesture like this and end up looking even weaker than you already thought? Why would you humble yourself? Haven't you already tasted humility? Want more?

As for friends and family, they don't need to read your letter. You will not feel better if your best friend knows you are suffering. You're going to have to be a man and get through these moments.

I don't know if you've noticed, but we feel embarrassed if a person close to us shows signs of weakness. We do not want to see the weak, we do not want to see them vulnerable, we do not feel good in that situation, and we try to avoid it.

Consider that you just told your ex what you had to say and throw away the letter! Every time you have something to say to your ex, take out a piece of paper and a pen, but make sure all the letters end up in the same place, in the trash.


## 9. What did you do today to become better?

Late tonight, when you get home, you'll see all kinds of people. You'll see men drinking beer at the corner bar. In front of the stairs, teenagers waiting for the summer season to pass.

On the stairs two neighbors are discussing why the rent is so high. As you climb the stairs, you will meet various neighbors, each with their way of wasting their lives, each with their vice, each with their excuse for not being who they would have wanted to be.

If I were the one to come home and see you, would I put you in the above categories? What would I think of you? Would you get rid of my criticism? Could I consider you worthy of appreciation, or would I look down on you and despise you?

And yes, I know I'm quick to label people, and I don't take all the data into account, but guess what? Even the woman who will pass by you tomorrow will not waste time taking all the data into account. She'll get an idea of you in a split second, and if you don't get a passing grade, you'll only have a chance at her if you start believing in reincarnation.

By the way, I know the idea that you should live your life without caring about the opinions of others. Very good idea, but it doesn't work. Or it works until you reach an age and you get tired of complaining that you can't find a quality woman.

Don't be fooled, quality women, the ones you are looking for, have standards, have mandatory minimum requirements, and are looking for quality men. They have a list of qualities they want in a man, and they will try to find the suitor who ticks the most points on the list.

And I'm not talking about those women who ask a lot from a man, although they have nothing to offer. Those women live in their fairytale world until they reach the age of 35 alone and start blaming men for not finding anyone. No, I'm talking about those women who have something to offer and who deserve to have a place in your life.

It's nice to dream that such a woman will fall in love with us for the way we are and that it will be love at first sight, but the reality is a little different. The reality is that you are a product, and like any product, you have to know how to sell yourself. If you are not the best option, you have little chance.

If you go to the supermarket to shop for the whole week, but you only have 100 dollars in your pocket, you will not put the first products that come your way in the basket. You will calculate your needs and options very well, and you will make the best decisions. You will not allow yourself to buy everything you want, but you will try to buy as many products as possible with that money.

Every woman has her value, which decreases over time, so she tries to attract the male with the most qualities she can conquer and is not satisfied with the first man who gets in her way.

So, if your ideal woman walks past your stairs and you enjoy the benefits of beer along with the other male friends, you've just missed the chance of a lifetime.

What could you do? Very much! Did you read any books today? Not literature, it would be preferable to learn something from that book. Have you ever been to a movie with yourself to get used to having fun on your own? Have you tried to work a second job or open a small business after hours? Have you been to the gym to improve your fitness?

When you bought bread, did you talk to the saleswoman and make her laugh to work on your social skills and prepare for the moment when the woman of your dreams will be in front of you? Did you take care all day to pull your shoulders back and keep your chin up when you walk to gain confidence just because of your posture?

Have you talked to an expert in a field where you want to become an expert and try to capture as much information as possible? Did you do something today to be better than you were yesterday?

There is a lot to do, and in time, we will discuss them all, but you are not allowed to waste a single day until then. Make a list of things you want to change about yourself and start today. The road is long and deserted; you will see that everyone you see on the stairs every night has not started and will never start on this road.

That's why, if you stick to this path, you will become one of the best. What did you do today to get better?

## 10. Why don't you trust yourself after the divorce?

Because you're not good enough for your ex-wife and your subconscious knows that. And I'm not telling you because I'm wrong or I have something to do with you, but the market makes the price, and the market has just shown you that your ex-wife doesn't want to buy what you sell.

Here you would have wanted me to be a motivational speaker and tell you that you are good enough for her, you have to believe in yourself, but I don't see what you gain if I lie to you and let you live in your bubble, far away of the real world.

Why am I so sharp with you? Firstly because it is true, secondly, today, you realize that you are not good enough for her is not necessarily bad. Maybe you should wake up and join us in real life.

Maybe you met in high school, and it was love at first sight. Maybe your plans for the future were limited to just graduating. Maybe you were on the same level. But it is just as possible that today she will be a Senior PR Specialist at that top multinational, and you will be a taxi driver.

I'm not saying it's terrible that you do taxi, I'm saying that you have to be content with a woman who wants a relationship with a taxi driver. Your ex-wife wants a relationship with someone who is at least at her level. And it's not her fault. This is the world we live in, and it's normal to be like that.

Have you seen many doctors marrying painters? But women with good jobs in corporations who marry unskilled construction workers? Although there may be such cases, women will generally look for men they can respect. And to respect them, those men must have accomplished at least as many things in life as they did.

In short, you need to show value constantly. If you do not rise to your wife's level, someone will rise to that level.

You will soon understand that women do not want an equal from you, a companion. They want a leader, a pioneer. They want to have physical and mental security. They want to know that if the third world war comes tomorrow, you will find a solution so that she and the potential child do not suffer at all. Were you that man?

Another case would be that your housewife, whom you maintained for years and paid for sessions at the hairdresser, the manicure, the anti-cellulite massage, would have found someone else. I'm sorry for you, but the new guy certainly looks more valuable than you. Maybe he has a better job, better prospects, or an honest man, and you are a scared child who treats his wife as his mother.

Regardless of the difference between you, she chose him because he is more valuable than you.

Unfortunately for you, your wife has decided that she can attract someone better in her life. You wouldn't stay with her either if it didn't live up to your expectations, even if your expectations have recently multiplied, or even if your expectations are unrealistic.

If you're not hypocritical, you may have the courage to admit that if you had won the lottery last year, the first thing before selling your old car would have been to start looking around for women who look much better than your wife.

When we want to get rid of the old laptop, its value is not given by the price we ask; the value is given by the amount the final buyer is willing to pay. In your case, your wife didn't want to pay the price you asked for, even though it once seemed like a reasonable price.

And yet, what has changed, and what can you do now?

Many things could change, but broadly speaking, your value as a man has not kept pace with hers. Perhaps her value as an individual has increased through personal development. Maybe she was able to attract someone more valuable in her life. Or maybe you fell in her eyes because you didn't behave like a man.

What you need to understand is that instinct does not deceive you. Suppose you feel inferior to her or her new boyfriend. In that case, you are inferior, and you also know which part you are inferior to.

Why is it a good thing? Well, there was a saying that the first step to healing is to admit that you have a problem. Congratulations, you just stopped being a victim and started taking responsibility for what is happening in your life. It's damn hard to do that, and it's easy to blame her for everything.

When their wives abandon them for someone with a better financial situation, the vast majority of men disregard their ex-wives. Few take into account the fact that perhaps the new financial situation of the new type is the result of years of hard work.

Maybe he didn't neglect college. Maybe when others came home and watched football, he had a second job. Maybe when others paid to get a warm job, he worked 12 hours a day, six days a week on his small business. He may have accomplished something while others complained that the state did not give them anything. He may be an honest, brave, strong-willed man with a purpose in life while others weep when their wives abandon them and beg her on their knees to reconcile.

Few want to understand that their ex-wives respect their new guys and not them for various reasons, and just as few want to understand that the new guy is over them in at least one chapter.

What to do? You have to become that guy, even better than him. You need to analyze yourself correctly and see where you have shortcomings and work on them. Maybe your career is not your strong point, but it will have to become. Maybe you lack ambition, but you will have to discover it. Maybe you didn't behave like a man, and you were weak.

No matter where you went wrong, you can work on that chapter to become the best version of yourself. It can take you a month, it can take you a year, but if you understand where you went wrong today, it will be difficult for you to repeat the same mistake, and it will be much harder to wake up again in the situation of being abandoned.

It's good to develop, it's great to try to become the best version of yourself, it's good that you want to be over the new guy. Don't try to reconquer your ex-wife, you just struggle until you no longer feel inferior, after which you continue your development far above its level.

If you don't go this hard way to find someone far above your ex-wife's level, you haven't gone the right way!


## 11. Are you afraid of loneliness?

If so, then you will have to learn to be alone. This step is important and will determine your future. How? Well, suppose you don't learn to feel good outside of a relationship. In that case, you will always try to get in the first relationship that gets in your way, and even you know that's not a good thing.

In the immediate future, while the wound of a divorce is still open, you will tend to reconcile with your ex and forgive many unforgivable things just to stop the pain caused by loneliness.

Most of the time, the fear of separation arises at divorce or separation, especially since the divorce comes after many years spent together. It's normal, and there's nothing wrong with feeling that, it's wrong to capitulate.

Your identity is closely linked to it. You were always together, and your friends always saw you "as a package". Now you feel weird, and you feel that part of you is missing. Yes, I know it's hard for you, and you don't know exactly who you are anymore, you feel that the world has turned you upside down, but that's it, you have to accept reality.

And the reality is that you have to reinvent yourself, you have to create that independent "John", untied through the umbilical cord by anyone. You don't know who this John is either, but let's think about it because we can create John ourselves, it doesn't have to be rediscovered.

What do I mean? John has always liked football, he also has a favorite team, but since he met his ex-wife, he hasn't been to matches for various reasons. His friends don't even know when they last saw him at a favorite team match.

"New" John goes to the stadium because he enjoys it. Friends look suspiciously at John's new passion, but that doesn't discourage him because the "new" John is convinced that he only has to do what pleases him.

When talking about new passions, John is careful not to blame anyone for not trying them earlier. John knows that the only culprit is himself for not knowing how to impose himself in the relationship. John has just learned that it is important to keep the hobbies and activities we had before the relationship in a relationship.

Everything you neglected, everything you wanted to try, you can try now. Go to concerts alone, go to the theater alone, go to the movies alone, go to art exhibitions, whatever makes you happy, and you know what? You will feel strange. You will have the impression that people look at you strangely and judge you.

I guarantee you will be among the only people in the cinema who came alone. Suppose you are stubborn like me to sit in the last row, next to the entrance to the cinema. In that case, I guarantee you that it will seem to you that everyone who enters the hall will look at you strangely and feel that they are judging you.

At the theater, you will be the only one without a friend or a partner. You will feel that you stand out, and it will probably be so because you do not feel good in your skin, which is seen in the behavior.

Alone at a three-day music festival? Have you ever considered doing this? Wouldn't you like to go alone to the one-hour concert? But to travel alone? To leave the country for a few days just you and the backpack? Have you ever thought about that? I don't think so, but it will be good to start thinking about that too.

Do a simple exercise and analyze people. If you don't dare to go to the festival alone, go to a concert and look for single people to analyze them, regardless of gender. You will find few because we are still friendly beings, but I hope you will find some.

Now, watch their behavior, and you will notice two types of people. You will see people who seem to be waiting for someone. Who feel embarrassed by the fact that they are alone at the concert. Those who are agitated and their attention is not only on the stage but also on the people in their immediate vicinity or on the phone.

If you are lucky, you will also find people who feel good in their skin as people who come to the concert alone. You will see that they are calm, attentive to the scene, and even have fun. They don't need anyone else to have fun.

You will see that those people have high self-confidence and somehow you will feel attracted to them. You will want to make friends with such a person because they will convey their calmness and peace of mind.

Why go to concerts, festivals, movies, and plays alone? Because you want to become that calm person who can have fun on his own. You want to become someone who doesn't need anyone's validation to be what he wants to be.

Women know how to read body language and the level of confidence they have in themselves. And self-confidence is gained by practicing it, not just reading this book or sitting in front of the computer. It is won on the street, at the concert, at the movie, at the theater. It is gradually gained, little by little, sometimes it is lost, but we must persevere.

However, there are many ways to gain self-confidence, and this is just one of them, but it is necessary, and it is good not to skip it.

In time you will find another woman, but still, it may not be suitable. You will have some question marks and some dissatisfaction. Suppose at that moment you will be a person who is not afraid to be alone. In that case, you will end the relationship, and you will look for someone who will tick all your requirements and criteria.

If not, you will prefer to stay in that relationship and accept the shortcomings because you will not want to be alone again and go through a breakup again. I don't think it makes sense to say the ideal scenario here.

When you finally find the right person for you, your behavior will differentiate between a failure and a successful relationship. A strong emotional man will give the woman enough space to choose him, reconciling with the idea that he may not be chosen.

A man who does not know how to be alone, who needs a relationship for validation, will do his best to conquer it, will suffocate it with attention, and the answer is inevitably the same, the woman moves away from him. She chooses the one who does not put pressure on her.

The quote that marked me the most lately is from Corey Wayne, and it says, "the strongest negotiating position is being able to walk away and mean it!". It applies to absolutely all areas of life, including married life.

Why is it important to be able to get up from the negotiating table and leave? Because you will be able to ask exactly what you want from a relationship. If you were honest with yourself, you would admit that in your relationship with your ex-wife, there were things that bothered you, but that you didn't say because you didn't want to argue, or you didn't want to make her suffer, or that you didn't think you could get.

When you dare to ask for what you want from a partner, but at the same time you will be able to give up the relationship if you do not get what you want, then you will see what power has a man who is not afraid to be single.

In most cases, you will get what you asked for, and it's not about manipulation, it's not about hidden games, you're not doing anything against her, because she wants a strong guy, she wants to see you capable of asking clearly what you want.

She may make a direct concession to you by accepting your requirements, but she has just won a strong man, and that makes her feel safe, makes her feel feminine, makes her feel attractive to you.

And yet, the main reason you need to learn to feel good outside of a relationship is another. You will be able to get over the divorce more quickly, you will no longer think obsessively about how to get the ex back, you will not get home praying that the house will not be empty.

You will end up being enough for your happiness. You will come to feel that your happiness is not attached and conditioned by anyone but you. And it will be fantastic, I promise. As long as you don't need anyone else to be happy, you control your life, and it's a rare thing these days. You are enough!

Loneliness didn't kill anyone. Fear of loneliness, yes!

## 12. Why do you need to learn to say "NO"

Strong people have things in common. Wealthy people have things in common. But better speaking, they have common character traits. They are quite similar in many ways. In all strong people, you will find the ease they can say "no" to someone.

I don't think it lasted 3 seconds, and you have already categorized those who are used to saying "no" as being, let's put it nicely, less pleasant people. I don't know if you're wrong, many are in that category, and many are conscious and committed. But if you have the impression that pleasant entrepreneurs like Elon Musk or Richard Branson have a problem refusing you, you are sorely mistaken.

We often find ourselves in unpleasant situations that we could have avoided if we had put our foot in the door and said no. A co-worker asks you to help him move, a co-worker asks you to help her with a car problem, a neighbor wants you to help him with something that seems useless, but it is ultra-important for him. Is it worth taking care of all Saturday? He is retired and has nothing better to do. But you? You're stupid!

Out of a stupid desire to please everyone (a psychologist will also explain where you get this desire from), you agree to help them, you accept that their problems become your problems, you put your desires back in the last place, and you prove to your subconscious that you don't matter.

A moving colleague can turn to a specialist company. Why do you help him? What do you have to gain from this? Will you ever need him, and he will immediately jump to your aid? Probably not. And then?

Is it that bad if you use that Saturday to do the things you want to do for a long time but postpone them? Is it that bad if you use it to sleep and recover from the chronic fatigue accumulated lately? Is it that bad if you prefer to read a book?

If the repair on your colleague's car takes more than a few minutes or is quite complex, there are services. You're not a mechanic. I know you want to please your colleague, but you won't gain anything by playing the role of the servant.

And yes, I am well aware that you feel a little outraged now, and you don't understand how I can be so selfish, but let me shatter your dreams. The real world is not that corner of heaven you believe in, and your model of society is just a utopia. In real life, people use you. Sometimes consciously, sometimes unconsciously, but they certainly use you. Just as you constantly use them.

And I want to explain something interesting to you, something that the kind of thing in you hasn't understood until now. If you refuse the colleague who asks you to change a light bulb in his car, he will not hate you. He will respect you because you know how to push your limits, and respect leads to attraction. So, in the end, it seems a bit illogical, although it is not, you will like it more. I know it's hard to believe or understand at first, so I'll let you re-read this paragraph.

Why is this happening? Because the servants are not sexy. If you try to be her servant, she will not respect you because you do not respect yourself. If you go down to the level of car mechanic for her, you remain only her car mechanic.

On the street, a very beautiful and provocatively dressed woman tries to change a light bulb in the car. A hundred men pass her. How many of them offer to help her?

A few meters further, a woman with whom nature has not been as great tries to change the same light bulb in the car. And a hundred men pass by her. Is the number of men who offer to help her equal to the number of men who help the first woman? Of course not. Why?

Because the idea that we help each other because it's so lovely of us is just a lie, we help our fellow human beings because we want something, either from them or from us. Consciously or unconsciously, when we help, we want something back.

Even men who help the less beautiful woman do it because they want to feel better in their skin and tell themselves that they are good people, essential members of society, to sleep peacefully at night. Good people will go to heaven. Karma never sleeps, and this good deed will come back to them when they need it most. Some will play the lottery later.

We don't know how to say NO because we want to be liked by others. We want so much to be considered good people by those around us that we break our standards and limits, do not respect ourselves at all, and then wonder why those around us do not respect us.

And don't get me wrong. Some people deserve it. Some people would turn your gesture around without blinking. Some people are really by your side and whose friendship is precious to you. In this case, you will carry furniture on the stairs on Saturday morning.

And you will do it to make you feel good knowing that you will end up in heaven, or you will do it because you want to be friends with that person. Whatever the reason, you have to do it.

What I want from you is to respect yourself. Respect your time and do not waste it helping your neighbor fix his car when he could go to the mechanic. Never agree to do things you don't want to do for people who don't deserve it, for whatever reason. You can't be everyone's friend, and it's not good to be everyone's friend.

The subject is very complex, and there are many nuances that I hope to touch on in the following sub-chapters, but in order not to become boring, I say so much: do not lie! Don't shake your head with elaborate excuses for not being able to dedicate the whole weekend to the noble cause of your co-worker. An "I'm sorry, I can't. I already have other plans "is enough.

And that plan can be a 12-hour mini-coma to get rid of fatigue. Or a Netflix marathon, or what the hell makes you happy because you're a man, and you don't have to explain to anyone how you spend your free time.


## 13. Why does body posture increase your self-confidence?

Keep your head up! And this is not an inspirational message, but from today we begin to pay attention to the posture of our body. If you still want to gain confidence, start here.

The idea is simple, people who keep their heads up and their chests forward are dominant. You know that I don't have to tell you. And yet, why do I say it? Because I don't think you're aware of how much your self-confidence increases when walking down the street, lifting your chin, and pushing your chest forward, even if you have no reason to.

You have to do it. Even if you had a hard day and feel tired, angry, or insecure about yourself. No matter how you feel, the simple fact that you walk with your head up and your chest in front of you will change your condition.

Why? Because it takes strength to do that. Do an experiment and while you are in a public place, pull your shoulders back so that your chest comes forward. How do you feel then? Do you feel vulnerable? Do you feel more exposed? It's not that easy to keep your chest in front, is it? Well, from today, you will have to control your body position.

And I know you won't succeed at first. Just because I wrote you what to do here does not mean that you will always stand with your head up and your chest in front. All I want from you is to try a few times to pay attention to your posture and correct it if necessary. How many times? Until you see the benefits.

And the benefits come for sure because that's not a trick. You will not fool your mind into believing that you are stronger than you are just because you hold your chest in front of you. In fact, at that moment, you feel vulnerable, you feel unprotected, and you become stronger because you get out of your comfort zone, just like a child who is afraid of the dark but decides to walk on an unlit street.

To do this, he needs courage, and it is normal for him to feel brave and strong in the end. So if you take your chest out in front, keep your head up and get over the insecurity that is trying you, it's called that you just got courage. You just had the strength to walk exposed, unprotected on the street, and that made you feel better in your skin.

Why do this? Because you want to feel good in your skin, and women notice that from miles away. Yes, I remind you that women are very attentive to what we communicate non-verbally. And you know what a man who keeps his head up and his chest in front of it conveys non-verbally.

What else do I want from you? Read people. Look, at a party, someone is constantly embarrassed by the fact that they don't know anyone, and they will inevitably have their hands in front of their chests.

When the boss lectures an employee for something he has done wrong, you will see that he tends to take a defensive stance, puts his hands in front of his body, or finds a file or anything else to cover his chest, or straightens his body.

Turn this into a game. Can you read a man only from his position? The more you play with people's reading, the more importance you will give to this, and correct your body posture.

No matter how boring or unimportant the subject may seem to you, you have to admit that you know what man you hope to become, and it's hard for me to believe that man doesn't have strong body language. If you feel like you're going to become that man without working on it, you're wrong. You don't just win by reading books. You end up implementing what you read there so often that it becomes your second nature.

If you just realized that you have a lot of work ahead of you and you feel somehow overwhelmed, let me cry a little….. Done!

## 14. Why is it important to never look down?

Look into her eyes and don't look down. Whoever gives up first loses! It sounds like childish play, but it's not. It's very appropriate behavior. Your gaze is the first thing a woman looks at when she wants to see who you are.

Today you will learn an important thing, which will help you both in your relationships with women and your daily life. You will learn that you have to control your gaze in front of a woman, a client, a boss, or any other man.

Ideally, I should tell you that you have to maintain eye contact with the one in front of you, but you won't have James Bond's eyes tomorrow because I told you to do it here.

What I want from you, instead, is to be aware of your gaze. Why? Because until I learned how important it is, I never paid attention to this aspect. Until I learned about this, I was unaware that I look awkwardly at the ground when someone looks at me.

What do you have to do? Go for a walk. When someone comes from the opposite direction, look directly into their eyes and try not to be the one to move the gaze elsewhere. Whether you succeed or not, the idea is to be aware of how you feel in those seconds. You will feel the interaction as a confrontation, you will feel as in a duel. You will feel that it is a struggle with someone you do not know.

Many times you will give in and look down. It's not a problem, you can't succeed from the first night. It's important to ask yourself right away why you gave up. Why did you feel intimidated by the other person?

I want you to realize that the moment you looked away from the person in front of you, you did it because you felt weaker than her.

What do you have to learn from here? Now you understand why a girl who likes you looks deep into your eyes. He wants to see if you have the courage to look back. She wants to see if you have the strength if you're stronger than her. Whether she does it consciously or not, women test you.

Although I always say that women do not know what they want (PS: women do not know what they want), if you still ask them, many will tell you that they want a man who can trust,to be self-controlled. Well, if you didn't know how women realize if you're in control, find out that the look is the one that gives you a hard time from the first interaction.

If you don't dare to look her deep in the eye, what are you sending her? That you're intimidated by her? Are you afraid of her? What woman wants a man to be afraid of her?

In your walk through the park, you will meet several types of people. Some will not make eye contact for even a second, and that's because they are not interested in your existence. Some women will look down at the ground for a second and then look back at you. That's a sign that they are at least curious about who you are.

And you will meet confrontational people, like in a war of glances. I want the moment you find such a person to enter the game and win it. Under no circumstances will you be the one to look first.

And we come back to our questions. How do you feel at that moment? See how hard it is to be a winner in this game? That's why people with good eye contact are seen as powerful people, because they have to go through what you went through every day, with every person they meet. After you won your little game, how did you feel? Is it true that you felt stronger?

Well, this is a great trick to gain confidence. Even if you feel that you do not have the strength to win this game, do not give in and do not look down, and you will see that you will gain confidence.

You need to know that you don't just have to look into their eyes if you're talking to someone. It seems unnatural, and you will look weird.

You will have to find a balance, but under no circumstances will you look down (try to look sideways from time to time), not when you speak, but when the other person speaks, and try always to be aware of who dominates the conversation. No sense in telling you now - I don't want to ruin the surprise.

Zan Perrion (author of an excellent book, "The Alabaster Girl"), once asked an excellent question: „If you were in a bar and wanted to compliment a young lady's dress without being able to use words or hands, how would you do it?" You would use your eyes and smile, wouldn't you? So you can send messages with your eyes.

Then when you look deep into a woman's eyes, you have to send her more "Hello, I'm curious who you are" and less "I'm stronger than you, and I dominate you!" Look at me, what an alpha male I am. " It will be harder at first, but if no one calls the police, I say you're on the right track.

Now, you will have to understand that what you learn today will be useful for the rest of your life, from acquaintances to women, to work, when you negotiate something, when you try to sell something when you join a new team. See how others react to your gaze, and you will learn the power of eye contact in a person's life. A person who wants to start an argument with you can easily be discouraged by an intense look.

## 15. How to gain confidence in 7 simple steps?

Yes, titles like this are called clickbait and are made to attract you. Unfortunately, there is no magic formula for gaining confidence in yourself. Wouldn't it be cool to have a list of 7 things to do on a Sunday afternoon and go to work on Monday morning like James Bond?

You don't gain confidence in yourself on a Thursday night after work, it doesn't happen by chance, and those who do have it, didn't get it because "they are lucky". And frankly, self-confidence doesn't have an exact definition, and it's a rather complicated concept.

Why? A second league football player has self-confidence when he plays against a third league team and sees a match against a first league team as lost from the start. Can we say that he trusts himself? I do not know.

We get even more complicated if we think that the best football player in the world has massive confidence when he enters the field, and after the match, he stutters and blushes when he talks to a beautiful woman. Why? Because self-confidence is the belief that we can achieve what we set out to do. And this comes from two directions: from repetition or our value as human beings. Does it sound complicated? It is!

So as not to complicate matters, we return to you. As a divorced man, you are interested in gaining confidence that you will get through the divorce well, which means how long it takes to get back to normal, find someone else, or start a new family. The answer is simple: later, it takes time!

If you were in your fifth divorce and it was relatively easy to rebuild your life every time, then yes, you will rebuild your life pretty easy. If a hundred women passed through your bed before marriage, then yes, today you trust yourself because you know it's easy to find someone. If that's not your case, then you still have to wait.

If you want to trust yourself to talk to the girl you like, you will have to talk to many girls you like. Confidence comes from repetition. Suppose you initiate conversations with a hundred beautiful women. In that case, when you reach a hundred women, you will see that you are full of confidence because you have done it ninety-nine times before, and you have not died from it.

As I said above, trust also comes from your value as a human being. If you are successful in your career, you look good, you take care of your body, and you have masculine behavior, it is normal not to worry that you will find someone to take the place of your ex-wife.

What to do? You will have to practice. If you are interested in gaining confidence in interacting with women, you will need to interact with many women.

Do you want to trust yourself as a man? Learn to uphold your beliefs in front of others and don't give up when things get tough. Learn to be masculine, and after your masculinity is tested a few times, you will gain confidence. At the same time, evolve as a human being, and you will gain confidence. If you feel you deserve something, you will not doubt your ability to achieve that something.

How long does this take? Sometimes years. I know it's not what you want to hear, but some things can take years. Your luck is that this is not a game of all or nothing. Self-confidence is not something you either have or don't have. You will gain more and more confidence as you progress.

Another good thing is that there are all sorts of tricks to help you gain confidence, and we'll take them one at a time, but that doesn't mean you won't have to do the things that scare you.

As for women, you need confidence in yourself to conquer them, but you only gain confidence after conquering a few. I know life isn't fair, but in the beginning, you'll have to pretend.

Even if your soul trembles inside you, you will have to go to them as if you were James Bond. You will not feel James Bond, many women will catch you lying, but some will believe you, and every success will strengthen your faith.

Motivational speakers are suitable as an impulse to go beyond your limits, but you will not succeed on the couch. If you watch motivational videos, it will be easier for you to go and talk to the woman you like, but the trust will not come from that movie. It will come only after you have exceeded your comfort zone, just as my advice is useless if you don't put it into practice.

The conclusion? Videos help, inspirational quotes help, little tricks help, simulating trust helps. But the emptiness in the stomach disappears with work and courage and can last for years. If you still feel that you are not good enough, then you have not reached your destination. Keep going!

## 16. Why is it extremely important to live alone after divorce?

If, after the divorce, you are the one who has to find a new home, then you may have the winning ticket. I'm not saying that someone draws a winning lottery ticket in a divorce, but your lottery ticket is unlucky.

And I understand you perfectly if for a while you want to stay with your parents, friends or share the rent with other people. But that should only be temporary. And I don't advise you to do it.

You will never feel like a man if you cannot financially support yourself if you cannot afford your own home. After a divorce, you tend to have low morale and low self-esteem. How do you think your self-esteem will increase if you have to go home to your parents at the age of 35?

At some point, you will be ready to go out on dates. It doesn't matter that some women will ridicule you for staying with your parents at your age. If you know how to say it, you will find women who will understand the situation.

Instead, you do not have an intimate space where only the two of you can be. And you have to be aware that if you are already 30 years old, a woman will not just look at how you look. If she decides that she wants to be together, she wants to see that you can support a family. What message do you send when you stay at mom's house?

The real problem is that your psyche is tempted by everything happening to you now, and returning home to your parents is a failure that will not make you feel better in your skin.

And I know you need friends during this time, just as you need to feel close to your family. But I tell you from my own experience that you only need time spent with your thoughts. You need to be alone.

Maybe you want to discharge yourself emotionally without anyone seeing you, maybe you want to analyze what happened, or maybe you want to be sad for a whole day, without having to give explanations to anyone or without having to pretend to be good so that you don't worry about your parents.

I know you have a lot of expenses now, but make living alone a priority. And looking to the future, don't forget that I told you here that you will have to learn to feel good alone, and you won't learn that at home with mom.

As for your psyche, you may fall into the trap of seeing your parents return home as something temporary until the waters calm down and you reconcile with your ex-wife, while the right attitude would be to start over. And if you reconcile, you must see reconciliation as a bonus, not as a purpose in life.

My advice is simple: if you have to, save on cigarettes, fun, anything, and rent a house where you can start over. And somehow make her fully furnished because I don't want to hear you call her to ask if she needs the iron you forgot when you left.

## 17. The man turned into a housewife is boring, and the women do not like boredom.

Today's article is complicated. You may misunderstand it, so take a chair and read it quietly. Today I'm talking about how to be, and at the same time not be, a housewife.

Because there are two things, just as important, just as necessary, but just as contradictory. And it's your duty to find a balance. But it's not a lot of stress, because if you can't find that balance, you only lose your family.

If you want a somewhat normal relationship, you will have to do things around the house. As long as you both have a job, you both work from home after hours. I don't want to tell you what to do around the house, but you have to agree somehow.

Think that after eight hours of work, she can't come home to cook, wash and iron, vacuum, and in the end, change that socket she asks you to change from February. You again? You watch TV because it's something exciting and you don't feel like it. It may work for a while, but I don't think it will work in the long run.

So far, nothing outrageous, I hope you agree with me. But you have to watch out and not to transform into a domesticated male. The kind who does everything around the house. Always. And with pleasure.

You have to help her, that's for sure, but if you always do, you'll get bored. It sounds awful, but that's the truth, whether you like it or not. And women hate boredom.

It's nice to help your wife. She will feel appreciated, understood, and loved at the beginning. But the man who cleans the house all the time is not necessarily sexy. And that's very important.

A man who surprises his girlfriend with a dinner he cooked is sexy. A man who cooks every day, no. He is a loving, understanding man, and much more. She will brag to you, friends. But she won't get excited when she sees you put parsley in the stew.

Will she be grateful for your help? Of course. Until it becomes a habit. Until it becomes your responsibility. Doesn't that sound sexy?

And that's precisely what we do. The first time she cooks for us, we don't know how to thank her. Sometimes we can barely swallow what she cooked, but we declare ourselves excited and encourage her. After a few years, we wonder how she had the nerve not to make some dessert.

What should you do? If you feel that you are no longer appreciated for what you do, stop doing it. Or change something. Maybe this week, you don't feel like doing work around the house.

Maybe this weekend you can't clean the house because you're fishing with friends. You can do it next week. I know she wants you to stay home and clean. But cleanliness can wait. Your friends don't.

And if you have the impression that cleaning the whole house this weekend you will end up in her graces and maybe you will be lucky in the evening when you try your luck, I want to let you know that your horoscope predicts a great disappointment in the evening.

I've said it before. One of the most read books in recent years is "50 Shades of Gray, " which is no coincidence. This kind of book is precisely the female fantasy. I wish you success in finding the main character in that book to vacuum or cook every day.

Don't use extremes. I say find a balance. Help your wife or girlfriend without turning into a housewife, predictable and boring. Help her without allowing her to turn you into a man she would never have sex with.

## 18. Do you want her to tell you to pull her hair during sex?

If the woman needs to tell you what to do as a man, you are not brave enough for her. So from the start, you start badly.

But that's not the real reason why a woman doesn't teach you what to do in bed. The real reason is the simple fact that we, as men, are stupid.

Because only whores want intense sex, right? Only whores want to be dominated in bed, only whores need to be stimulated during sex and their brain, not just the genitals, right? If she's not behaving like a nun at the church, then she's a lowly woman, isn't she? If you answered yes to any of the above questions, give yourself two slaps!

You have to understand that women are sexual beings, just like you. And since you have much weirder sexual fantasies than you're not tell her, guess what? She has much more spicy sexual fantasies than she would like to admit to you.

And why does she refrain from showing you her sexual nature? Because you will judge her for that. Because you will catalog, and you will no longer want a relationship with her. Because you're stupid.

And yet, what are you doing? First of all, you accept that she is also a sexual being, not just you. Second, you stop considering stimulating her sexual organs as a prelude. Because, that's not an intro, you activate a reflex of her body made to protect the vagina from future sexual activity. That doesn't mean she's necessarily excited.

And third, you dominate her in bed. You act like a man and let her be a woman. And since any woman has the right to say no, if she's bothered by something you do, she'll tell you that. But you have to try.

If you want to do something and you don't know if she agrees with it, you do that thing and let her say no. You try, and as long as she doesn't turn you down, it means you're doing well.

And fourth, if you do this and discover new things about her sexual nature, don't judge her or disregard her for her desires. That's if you don't want to be the last time you see this part of her.


**19. Why does your wife have a headache when you feel like having sex?**

I have said several times here that a relationship is a game of power. Well, sex is also a power play. Think carefully about the sexual act itself. Mainly, the man dominates the woman, and the woman lets herself be dominated by him.

In order to spread her legs and receive you inside, she has to accept your masculinity, your strength. It is nothing but an act of submission to the man. And now begins your problem, because it will be difficult for a woman to obey a weak man.

When you act like a personal servant, do you think it is easy for her to obey you? A scared person who doesn't know how to impose himself in front of her? It does not work that way.

I'm not talking about the "macho men" who vacuum and do household chores in the hope of a sex party. Well, who should those women obey? A housewife?

What's so sexy about a man vacuuming? Why would you think your wife would get wet if you clean the house?

So to answer the title question, your wife has a headache when you feel like having sex because, at that moment, she's not attracted to you. Because she has more important things to do than have sex with you, like watching TV or doing anything else.

And yes, your wife also has hormones and needs sex. Maybe with all your mistakes, the sex game is happening. Maybe she's having sex with you even if she's no longer attracted to you, but that's not quality sex, that's not passion. That's just hormone regulation. Whether you're there or someone else is the same for her. On the contrary, she may be attracted to another.

And let me tell you something. You tried to start a sex game, and she refused. Do you think that if her favorite Hollywood actor is in the room, she would still have a headache? Do you think he would be rejected? Do you think she would explain to Keanu Reeves that she had a hard day and needs a good sleep? Do you think Jason Momoa would be turned down because she did not take a shower or she would be jumping in the shower in a second? Dude, you're her headache!

And the most important thing is the following. There may be some attraction in that relationship, but when you want it, she may not be in the mood. In this case, keep in mind that sex does not start in the evening, at bedtime.

Do not expect to be successful if you come home after a long day, eat, shower, go to bed, and then try to start a sex game. Sex starts in the morning when you wake up. Through your behavior, through sexual jokes, through foreplay, through everything you know that arouses her. In the evening, you only reap the results, but the work starts in the morning.

## 20. There will be always a better man than you.

If you are rich, there will be someone richer than you, if you have a good job, there will be a man with a better job than you. If you are successful in your business, there will always be someone who has a more significant business that grows faster. You will never be the best in a field, or if you are, it will not last indefinitely.

And what to do? It doesn't matter that you are not in the first place as long as you do your best to be in the first place.

This discussion occurs when you tell a man that it must be the best option for the woman next to him. Because guess what? He'll have to do this his whole life. He will have to struggle all his life for the woman next to him to look with admiration at what he represents as a man. And this is about you too.

Do I have a solution for you? No. Will I cry that you have such a burden on your shoulders? No. What is there to be done? You can't stay with fear that the woman next to you will leave with someone else. Honestly, you will have to understand that we men compete for success, just as women compete for the most beautiful woman in your life.

That's right, life is hard and complex, not like you thought as a child. The game is tough, but some win it, others lose it, but at least try, and others lose it by not showing up.

Is it possible that the woman next to you will leave you for someone else? Yes, of course. Does it make sense to think about that? No, it doesn't. As long as you do your best to become the best version of yourself, you don't have to think about it. Because it won't help you gain confidence. Because you will become suspicious and jealous. Because that's just fear, and that's not what a woman should see in you.

So, yes, it's hard to be a man, but I don't care. Get your hands on it and grow!

www.ingramcontent.com/pod-product-compliance
Lightning Source LLC
LaVergne TN
LVHW020927200726
843506LV00011B/1853